Lecture Notes in Computer Science   10107

Commenced Publication in 1973
Founding and Former Series Editors:
Gerhard Goos, Juris Hartmanis, and Jan van Leeuwen

More information about this series at http://www.springer.com/series/7409

Christian Berger · Mohammad Reza Mousavi
Rafael Wisniewski (Eds.)

Cyber Physical Systems

Design, Modeling, and Evaluation

6th International Workshop, CyPhy 2016
Pittsburgh, PA, USA, October 6, 2016
Revised Selected Papers

 Springer

Editors
Christian Berger
University of Gothenburg
Gothenburg
Sweden

Rafael Wisniewski
Aalborg University
Aalborg
Denmark

Mohammad Reza Mousavi
Halmstad University
Halmstad
Sweden

ISSN 0302-9743   ISSN 1611-3349   (electronic)
Lecture Notes in Computer Science
ISBN 978-3-319-51737-7   ISBN 978-3-319-51738-4   (eBook)
DOI 10.1007/978-3-319-51738-4

Library of Congress Control Number: 2017930211

LNCS Sublibrary: SL3 – Information Systems and Applications, incl. Internet/Web, and HCI

Printed on acid-free paper

This Springer imprint is published by Springer Nature
The registered company is Springer International Publishing AG
The registered company address is: Gewerbestrasse 11, 6330 Cham, Switzerland.

Preface

Welcome to the proceedings of CyPhy 2016: the 6th International Workshop on Design, Modeling and Evaluation of Cyber Physical Systems, which was held on October 5, 2016, in Pittsburgh. This edition of CyPhy was held in conjunction with the Embedded Systems Week, which was organized during October 2–7, 2016, in Pittsburgh, USA.

For this edition, we received 14 submissions. All submission underwent a rigorous review process and each submission was reviewed by at least three, and on average more than four, Program Committee members. The committee decided to accept nine papers, which were presented in the workshop, and of which the revised versions appear in this proceedings volume.

In addition to the contributed papers and presentations, the program featured a keynote presentation by Dr. Jyotirmoy Deshmukh from Toyota. The keynote presentation, of which an abstract is included in this volume, skillfully integrated the scientific rigor of formal methods with the industrial complexity of cyber-physical systems in the automotive domain.

This was the sixth edition of CyPhy and we are glad to see that it has an established tradition and has found a stable place in the landscape of cyber-physical systems research venues.

We would like to gratefully acknowledge the effort of our distinguished Program Committee members for their extensive effort in reviewing papers and for helping us compose a high-quality program. We thank the additional reviewers for their review reports. We would like to thank the Steering Committee of CyPhy and its general chair, Walid Taha, for their help, support, and confidence.

We express our best thanks to Ferenc Bartha and Scott Hissam for having chaired the CyPhy 2016 sessions. We appreciate the valuable contribution of EasyChair and Springer in the seemless organization of the submission, review, and publication processes.

November 2016

Christian Berger
Mohammad Reza Mousavi
Rafael Wisniewski

Organization

Program Committee

Christian Berger	University of Gothenburg, Sweden
Manuela Bujorianu	University of Strathclyde, UK
Thao Dang	CNRS/VERIMAG, France
Scott Hissam	Software Engineering Institute, USA
Daisuke Ishii	University of Fukui, Japan
Mehdi Kargahi	University of Tehran, Iran
Zhiyun Lin	Zhejiang University, China
Mohammad Reza Mousavi	Halmstad University, Sweden
Enrico Pagello	University of Padua, Italy
Mihaly Petreczky	École des Mines de Douai, France
Michel Reniers	Eindhoven University of Technology, The Netherlands
Bernhard Rumpe	RWTH Aachen University, Germany
Maytham Safar	Kuwait University, Kuwait
Christoph Seidl	Technische Universität Braunschweig, Germany
Christoffer Sloth	Aalborg University, Denmark
Jonathan Sprinkle	University of Arizona, USA
Martin Steffen	University of Oslo, Norway
Frits Vaandrager	Radboud University Nijmegen, The Netherlands
Rafael Wisniewski	Aalborg University, Denmark

Additional Reviewers

Carraro, Marco	Lachmann, Remo	von Wenckstern, Michael
Chaki, Sagar	Schroeder, Jan	
Eikermann, Robert	Schulze, Christoph	

Formal Methods for Cyber-Physical Systems in the Automotive Domain (Extended Abstract)

Jyotirmoy Deshmukh

Toyota Technical Center, Gardena, CA, USA
jyotirmoy.deshmukh@toyota.com

Introduction

Systems where the behavior of a *physical* aspect of the system, such as that of a mechanical component is controlled using embedded software (*i.e.*, the "*cyber*" component) are called *cyber-physical systems*. A modern vehicle is an example of a complex cyber-physical system with burgeoning software size and complexity [2]. There are many exciting things on the horizon for the automotive domain, including advanced driver assist systems, self-driving cars, intelligent transportation systems, and alternative fuel sources. These advances can only further increase the complexity of embedded automotive software. Thus, it is imperative for the embedded software design process to recognize the challenges posed by increasing software complexity.

The problem of checking if all behaviors of a general cyber-physical system satisfy a behavioral property, for even a simple class of such properties is a very hard problem [3]. The *de facto* standard in industrial design, especially when faced with models such as those in [8], is to rely on rigorous testing, either at the level of system models or on the physical implementation of the system. However, a key challenge in such testing is that test scenarios and expected outcomes are often described (formally or informally) in natural language. Thus, engineers often rely on insight and experience to visually inspect test results to judge the performance of their designs. In what follows, we introduce a formal testing methodology that seeks to replace manual knowledge with machine-checkable requirements.

Requirement-Based Testing

Engineers often specify a scenario or setting for performing a test. These "conditions" are often specifications of allowable ranges for environmental factors (*e.g.*, ambient temperature, pressure, *etc.*), or patterns of driving behavior (*e.g.*, how often and how long a driver applies the brake). Then the engineers stimulate the system using an input signal satisfying the scenario specification and make a "judgement" about the output signal observed in relation to the applied input. This is analogous to the practice of specifying pre- and post-conditions on program behavior in the traditional literature on program verification. The key difference is that the pre- and post-conditions here can specify temporal behaviors of entire time-varying signals. Finding input signals satisfying arbitrary pre-conditions is generally challenging, but this problem can be mitigated by defining a parameterized input signal generator that produces a set of distinct input signals, all satisfying the given pre-condition. One approach to generate such signals is used by tools such as S-TaLiRo [1] and Breach [6], that use control points and a user-specified interpolation scheme to generate time-varying signals.

Post-conditions can often be reduced to designers looking for certain patterns in the output signals. Control engineers typically look for properties such as rise times, settling times, overshoots, undershoots, spikes/glitches, oscillatory behavior, and timed causal relations between signals. Several of these patterns can be elegantly expressed using Signal Temporal Logic (STL). Recently, we proposed a library called ST-Lib (Signal Template Library) that represents a subset of STL (and mild extensions) that can capture some of these signal patterns. Using STL or a similar real-time temporal logic has the advantage that it is often possible to define quantitative semantics for such logics. Such semantics map a given post-condition requirement and a trace to a real number. Without loss of generality, the semantics can be defined such that a positive number indicates that the trace satisfies the requirement, while a negative number indicates that the trace violates the requirement, and the spectrum of numbers from positive to negative indicate the degree of satisfaction or violation. This enables the use of global optimization-based techniques or other heuristic search techniques to be employed for automatic test generation and falsification of given system models [1, 3, 6, 7], as well as techniques to mine requirements from models [9, 10].

Conformance Testing

In the model-based development (MBD) paradigm, designers can have a variety of models differing in the level of detail, but representing the same underlying system. In such a setting, it is useful to have a technique to compare different models; model conformance is such a technique that seeks to provide quantitative notions of model similarity. Given a bound δ and a distance metric d on the space of signals, we say that two models are δ-conformant under the distance metric d, if for each input signal, stimulating the two models with this signal results in output signals less than δ distance apart (using the distance metric d to define distance). While several distance metrics have been defined in the literature, we consider the Skorokhod metric. This metric allows comparing signals both in time and value space [4], has efficient computational algorithms, and preserves the order of events in signals when comparing them. Recently, we presented a falsification-based algorithm that seeks to maximize the Skorokhod distance between two model outputs, and thus test models for conformance [4, 5].

Research Challenges

Below we enumerate some of the grand challenges for formal methods for cyber-physical systems in general, and for automotive systems in particular:

1. Modeling physical phenomena using high-fidelity models that can be efficiently simulated is a challenge. Physics-based parametric models have the disadvantage that they need careful tuning to match actual data. An alternative is to use data-driven models, but accuracy and interpretability continues to remain a concern.
2. Though specifying formal requirements with temporal logic has allowed us to make some strides in requirement elicitation, the general problem of specifying requirements continues to be a challenge. A key issue is that control designers often are not trained in temporal logic and prefer formalisms such as frequency-domain properties or statistical metrics. An ongoing challenge is to design a suitable language that allows designers to express all their desired requirements in an intuitive fashion, while being expressive enough.
3. Cyber-physical system designers are faced with a data deluge problem due to copious amounts of monitoring information available. A challenge is to provide tools that can expose intrinsic structure in massive amounts of time-series data, perform supervised learning and clustering, and algorithms for anomaly detection. A bigger challenge is to learn artifacts that are logically interpretable by designers, rather than black-box classifiers (that are typical in standard machine learning algorithms).

Conclusion. In this extended abstract, we present a few in-roads that techniques based on formal methods have been able to make in the domain of automotive cyber-physical systems. We suggest that a testing framework based on formalizing requirements using temporal logic has a higher degree of automation compared to traditional testing practices. We introduce the problem of conformance testing and conclude with some grand challenges.

Acknowledgements. The author would like to acknowledge his colleagues at Toyota including James Kapinski, Xiaoqing Jin, Hisahiro Ito, Jared Farnsworth, and Ken Butts, and co-authors on the papers cited in this paper.

References

1. Annapureddy, Y.S.R., Liu, C., Fainekos, G.E., Sankaranarayanan, S.: S-TaLiRo: a tool for temporal logic falsification for hybrid systems. In: Abdulla, P.A.A., Leino, K.R.M. (eds.) TACS 2011. LNCS 6605, pp. 254–257 (2011)
2. Charette, R.N.: This car runs on code. IEEE Spect. **46**(3), 3 (2009)
3. Deshmukh, J.V., Jin, X., Kapinski, J., Maler, O.: Stochastic local search for falsification of hybrid systems. In: Finkbeiner, B., Pu, G., Zhang, L. (eds.) ATVA 2015. LNCS 9364, pp. 500–517 (2015)
4. Deshmukh, J.V., Majumdar, R., Prabhu, V.: Quantifying conformance using the skorokhod metric. In: Kroening, D., Păsăreanu, C.S. (eds.) CAV 2015. LNCS 9207, pp. 234–250 (2015)
5. Deshmukh, J.V., Majumdar, R., Prabhu, V.: Quantifying conformance using the skorokhod metric. Formal Methods in System Design (accepted for publication) (2016)
6. Donzé, A.: Breach, a toolbox for verification and parameter synthesis of hybrid systems. In: Touili, T., Cook, B., Jackson, P. (eds.) CAV 2010. LNCS 6174, pp. 167–170 (2010)
7. Dreossi, T., Dang, T., Donzé, A., Kapinski, J., Jin, X., Deshmukh, J.V.: Efficient guiding strategies for testing of temporal properties of hybrid systems. In: Havelund, K., Holzmann, G., Joshi, R. (eds.) NFM 2015. LNCS 9058, pp. 127–142 (2015)

8. Jin, X., Deshmukh, J.V., Kapinski, J., Ueda, K., Butts, K.: Powertrain control verification benchmark. In: Proceedings of Hybrid Systems: Computation and Control, pp. 253–262 (2014)
9. Jin, X., Donzé, A., Deshmukh, J.V., Seshia, S.A.: Mining requirements from closed-loopcontrol models. In: Proceedings of Hybrid Systems: Computation and Control (2013)
10. Jin, X., Donzé, A., Deshmukh, J.V., Seshia, S.A.: Mining requirements from closed-loop control models. IEEE Trans. Comput. Aided Des. Integr. Circ. Syst. **34**(11), 1704–1717 (2015)

Contents

A Model-Driven Framework for Hardware-Software Co-design
of Dataflow Applications 1
  Waheed Ahmad, Bugra M. Yildiz, Arend Rensink, and Mariëlle Stoelinga

Symbolic Analysis of Hybrid Systems Involving Numerous Discrete
Changes Using Loop Detection. 17
  Kenichi Betsuno, Shota Matsumoto, and Kazunori Ueda

SysML to NuSMV Model Transformation via Object-Orientation 31
  *Georgiana Caltais, Florian Leitner-Fischer, Stefan Leue,
  and Jannis Weiser*

CyFuzz: A Differential Testing Framework for Cyber-Physical Systems
Development Environments 46
  Shafiul Azam Chowdhury, Taylor T. Johnson, and Christoph Csallner

Ardán: Using 3D Game Engines in Cyber-Physical Simulations
(Tool Paper). 61
  Fergus Leahy and Naranker Dulay

Proving Correctness of Refactorings for Hybrid Simulink Models
with Control Flow. 71
  *Sebastian Schlesinger, Paula Herber, Thomas Göthel,
  and Sabine Glesner*

Automated Verification of Switched Systems Using Hybrid Identification ... 87
  Stefan Schwab, Bernd Holzmüller, and Sören Hohmann

Ontological Reasoning as an Enabler of Contract-Based Co-design 101
  *Ken Vanherpen, Joachim Denil, Paul De Meulenaere,
  and Hans Vangheluwe*

CPS Specifier – A Specification Tool for Safety-Critical
Cyber-Physical Systems. 116
  Jonas Westman, Mattias Nyberg, and Oscar Thydén

Author Index 127

A Model-Driven Framework
for Hardware-Software Co-design
of Dataflow Applications

Waheed Ahmad, Bugra M. Yildiz$^{(\boxtimes)}$, Arend Rensink, and Mariëlle Stoelinga

University of Twente, Enschede, The Netherlands
{w.ahmad,b.m.yildiz,arend.rensink,m.i.a.stoelinga}@utwente.nl

Abstract. Hardware-software (HW-SW) co-design allows to meet system-level objectives by exploiting the synergy of hardware and software. Current tools and approaches for HW-SW co-design face difficulties coping with the increasing complexity of modern-day application due to, e.g., concurrency and energy constraints. Therefore, an automated modeling approach is needed which satisfies modularity, extensibility and interoperability requirements. Model-Driven Engineering (MDE) is a prominent paradigm that, by treating models as first-class citizens, helps to fulfill these requirements. This paper presents a state-of-the-art MDE-based framework for HW-SW co-design of dataflow applications, based on synchronous dataflow (SDF) graph formalism. In the framework, we introduce a reusable set of three coherent metamodels for creating HW-SW co-design models concerning SDF graphs, hardware platforms and allocation of SDF tasks to hardware. The framework also contains model transformations that cast these models into priced timed-automata models, the input language of the well-known model checker UPPAAL CORA. We demonstrate how our framework satisfies the requirements of modularity, extensibility and interoperability in an industrial case study.

1 Introduction

Hardware-software (HW-SW) co-design is an engineering practice that allows to meet system-level objectives by exploiting the synergy of hardware and software through their simultaneous design. For instance, HW-SW co-design allows exploring design alternatives, and helps to improve the development cost and time-to-market. However, current tools and approaches for HW-SW co-design have difficulties coping with the concurrency and increasing complexity of modern-day systems. As a result, the time and effort needed for modeling and validating such designs are negatively affected. In fact, it has been widely recognized that a HW-SW co-design approach must have the following features [4,10,12,15] all of which are not satisfied by the current HW-SW co-designing approaches:

– *Modularity* [4,10]: The modeling approach should separate different aspects — such as hardware, software and their mappings — to keep their various

C. Berger et al. (Eds.): CyPhy 2016, LNCS 10107, pp. 1–16, 2017.
DOI: 10.1007/978-3-319-51738-4_1

concerns modular. This allows convenient exploration of design alternatives concerning hardware and software. Modules targeting different concerns are better maintainable and reusable.

– *Extensibility* [10]: The HW-SW co-designing approach should have convenient extension mechanisms allowing rapid implementation of possible future requirements. This reduces not only the development cost of new products, but also their time-to-market.

– *Interoperability* [4,15]: HW-SW co-designing often involves tools serving different purposes, such as model designing, simulating, integrating etc. The HW-SW modeling approach should support interoperability between these tools, enabling system designers to explore design alternatives rapidly.

Model-Driven Engineering (MDE) is an approach that helps to fulfill the aforementioned requirements [24]. In MDE, the important concepts of the target domain are formally captured in a so-called, *metamodel*. Separate metamodels for the domains of interest help to keep the design modular. All models are instances of a metamodel, or possibly an integrated set of metamodels. Moreover, models can be transformed to the other via *model transformations*, defined at the metamodel level.

In this paper, we model software applications as Synchronous Dataflow (SDF) graphs [16] which are partitioned into tasks, with inter-task dependencies. SDF graphs are well-known computational models for real-time streaming and dataflow applications. This paper presents a novel HW-SW co-design framework based on the principles of MDE. Our framework allows model-driven HW-SW co-designing of SDF applications mapped on multiprocessor hardware platforms, and generate energy-optimal schedules for these SDF applications. To generate energy-optimal schedules, our framework transforms the co-designed SDF and hardware models to priced timed-automata models. The problem of finding energy-optimal schedules (while satisfying minimal throughput requirements) is encoded as an optimization problem, defined as a reachability property over priced timed-automata models. The property is then checked by the model checker UPPAAL CORA [5] that generates an energy-optimal schedule.

Our framework consists of three metamodels: (1) a metamodel for SDF graphs; (2) a metamodel for Platform Application Models (PAMs), which describe the processor types and their power levels, and the cost of switching between the power levels; and (3) a metamodel for expressing potential allocations of the tasks in an SDF graph to the processor types in a PAM. As mentioned earlier, our framework considers the model checker UPPAAL CORA for generating energy-optimal schedules. Therefore, for supporting the generation of UPPAAL CORA models, we also use an existing UPPAAL metamodel developed at the University of Paderborn [1]. The models conforming to three metamodels explained earlier, are transformed to UPPAAL CORA models automatically via *model transformations* in the framework. We have already described our method of using priced timed-automata for the purpose of energy optimization in [2], and therefore out of scope of this paper. Rather the novelty of this paper is the design prospects of using MDE. Later in Sect. 5, we demonstrate our framework as an evidence to show the benefits of MDE namely, modularity, extensibility, and interoperability. The main contributions of this paper are as follows:

- We introduce the insights of state-of-the-art model-driven engineering approach into the embedded systems community, in particular for the domain of HW-SW co-design.
- We propose a reusable set of three coherent, extensible metamodels for HW-SW co-design.[1]
- We define and apply model transformations from the dataflow domain to the model-checking domain, obtaining an automated tool to compute energy-optimal schedules for dataflow applications.
- We demonstrate that our fully automated framework provides modularity, extensibility and interoperability between tools, via an industrial case study.

The rest of the paper is structured as follows: Sect. 2 provides the related work. Section 3 gives an overview of our framework and Sect. 4 describes the framework components in detail. Section 5 evaluates our framework using an industrial case study, and Sect. 6 concludes the paper.

The extended version of this paper can be found in the technical report [3].

2   Related Work

There exists a plethora of commercial and academic tools for HW-SW co-designing [4,6,9,10,12,15]. Here, we only present the closest studies.

The state-of-the-art toolsets in the realm of HW-SW co-design of dataflow applications, are Octopus [4] and Ptolemy [15]. The Octopus toolset [4], in comparison to our approach, does not consider any metamodels. Furthermore, this toolset uses Java libraries for model transformation. Rather than Java, which is a general-purpose language, we use ETL that is specifically designed as a domain-specific language for model transformations. The lack of metamodels and model transformation language cause challenges in extensibility and maintainability, which are in fact stated as a future directions of the work in [4]. Ptolemy [15] is another well-known toolset for supporting HW-SW co-design of dataflow applications. However, similar to Octopus, it is not based on MDE which poses challenges in reusability and maintainability.

The closest works to ours are presented in [6,9]. Both of these papers utilize MDE techniques for HW-SW co-designing of embedded systems. In contrast to our work, these papers consider generic software applications and hardware models. We, on the other hand, analyze real-life software applications and hardware models enabled with power management.

To the best of our knowledge, this paper presents the first model-driven HW-SW co-design framework for dataflow applications that provides modularity, interoperability, and extensibility.

---

[1] All metamodels, model transformations, and case studies discussed in this paper can be found at https://github.com/utwente-fmt/COMET. An instruction manual for replicating the experiments is also given in this repository.

3   The Model-Driven Framework

3.1   Model-Driven Engineering

Models are powerful tools to express behavior, structure and other properties in many domains such as mathematics, engineering, and other natural sciences. Model-Driven Engineering (MDE) is a software engineering approach that considers models not only as documentation, but also adopts them as the basic abstraction to be used throughout all engineering disciplines and in any application domain [7]. The models in MDE are closer to some particular domain concepts rather than the computing concepts. These models are considered equal to the code since they are formally defined and have execution semantics.

To define models, we need to specify their language as a model of these models at a more abstract level that is so-called *metamodels*. In their common use, metamodels capture the concepts of some domain or application; and define the permitted structure and behaviour, to which models must adhere. Therefore, metamodels describe the syntax of models [18].

MDE allows interoperability between different domains (and tools in these domains) via *model transformations*. Models transformations satisfy interoperability and furthermore save effort and reduce errors by automating the model derivation and modification process.

3.2   Overview of Model-Driven Framework

Figure 1 shows the detailed overview of our framework. The HW-SW co-design of the application consists of the first four steps:

– In step 1, an SDF model of the software application is created using the SDF³ tool [21] in an XML format specific to the tool.
– In step 2, the SDF model is transformed to an SDF model that conforms to the metamodel we defined for SDF graphs.
– In step 3, the hardware platform model is created using *PAM Visual Editor* that is a graphical editor for specifying Platform Application Models (PAMs). This model conforms to the PAM metamodel we defined for PAMs.
– In step 4, an allocation model is created for specifying the mapping of the tasks in the SDF model to the processor types in the PAM.

The analysis of the co-design for energy-optimal schedules is conducted using the UPPAAL CORA model checker. This is achieved in the last three steps:

– In step 5, the co-design is transformed to a priced timed-automata model that conforms to the UPPAAL metamodel.
– In step 6, the priced-timed-automata model is transformed to the format accepted by the model checker.
– In step 7, we analyze the resulting model to compute the energy-optimal schedule using the UPPAAL CORA model checker.

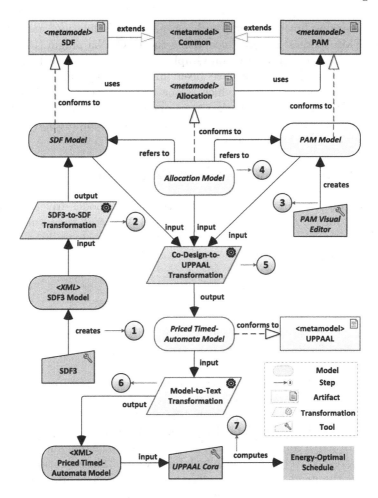

Fig. 1. Detailed overview of our framework. The elements with dark background color represent the new contributions.

Although the steps in Fig. 1 show a general guideline for a HW-SW co-design of a system from scratch, a different strategy can be adopted according to the requirements of the system design. For example, if a system designer needs to analyze how a software application runs on various hardware platforms, s/he can create an SDF model by follow steps 1 and 2 only once and then create several PAM models by conducting step 3 multiple times.

Detailed explanation of the framework are given in Sect. 4.

3.3   Tooling Choices

To realize the model-driven approach, we have created metamodels using ECore in Eclipse Modeling Framework (EMF) [19]. EMF provides a plethora of plugins to support various functionalities, such as querying, validation, and transformation of EMF models. For instance, using the EuGENia plugin [14], we have created PAM Visual Editor based on Graphical Editing Framework (GMF).

The model transformations have been implemented using Epsilon Transformation Language (ETL) [13], which is one of the domain-specific languages provided by the Epsilon framework. ETL supports many input-to-many output model transformations; it also allows the users to inherit, import and reuse other Epsilon modules in the transformations.

4   Details of the Model-Driven Framework

This section presents our concrete instantiation of the model-driven framework by describing our modeling choices in some detail. We recall the formal (mathematical) definitions of the domain concepts and discuss how we have chosen to translate them to metamodel elements.

4.1   SDF Graphs

Typically, real-time streaming applications execute a set of periodic tasks, which consume and produce a fixed amount of data. Such applications are naturally modeled as SDF graphs.

Definition and Metamodel. An SDF graph is a directed, connected graph in which tasks are represented by *actors*. Actors communicate with each other via streams of data elements, represented by *channels* (the streams) that carry *tokens* (an abstraction of the data elements). Each channel (a, b, p, q) connects a producer actor a to a consumer actor b, and specifies *production* and *consumption* rates p and q, respectively, both given by integer values. The execution of an actor a is known as the *firing* of a; as a result, q tokens are removed from any channel (b, a, p, q) of which a is the consumer, and q tokens are added to any channel (a, b, p, q) of which a is the producer. Formally:

Definition 1. *An* SDF *graph is a tuple* $G = (A, D, \mathsf{Tok}_0)$ *where A is a finite set of actors, $D \subseteq A^2 \times \mathbb{N}^2$ is a finite set of channels, and* $\mathsf{Tok}_0 : D \to \mathbb{N}$ *denotes the initial number of tokens on each channel.*

Some notation: given an SDF graph G as above, the sets of *input* and *output* *channels* of an actor $a \in A$ are defined respectively as $In(a) = \{(b, a, p, q) \in D \mid b \in A, p, q \in \mathbb{N}\}$ and $Out(a) = \{(a, b, p, q) \in D \mid b \in A, p, q \in \mathbb{N}\}$.

Example 1. Figure 2 shows the SDF graph of the Viola-Jones face detector [23], kindly provided by the company Recore Systems, that is used in their face recognition system. The SDF graph contains seven actors (*im_read*, *dupl_im*, *integral*, *haar_det*, *haar_scal*, *col_obj* and *grp_rect*) representing the tasks performed in face detection. For example, *im_read* captures the scene containing one or more faces, *haar_det* detects the regularities in the human face called *Haar features*, and *grp_rect* groups the rectangles having similar Haar features.

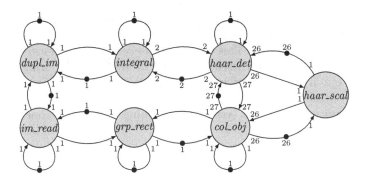

Fig. 2. SDF graph of Viola-Jones face detector

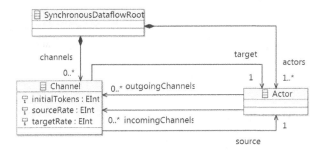

Fig. 3. SDF Metamodel

The *SDF Metamodel* capturing the concepts of Definition 1 is shown in Fig. 3. Recall that an SDF graph is a tuple $G = (A, D, \mathsf{Tok}_0)$.

- *SynchronousDataFlowRoot* is the root of a model, in which everything else is contained; it corresponds to G.
- *Actor* corresponds to the set A; the associations *incomingChannels* and *outgoingChannels* represent the derived functions *In* and *Out* from A to sets of channels.
- *Channel* corresponds to the set D. The 4-tuples $(a, b, p, q) \in D$ are represented in the metamodel by the *source* and *target* associations (for a and b), respectively the *sourceRate* and *targetRate* attributes (for p and q). *initialTokens* represents the function Tok_0; thus, it has been modeled as an attribute of *Channel*, rather than as a separate function.

With respect to the mathematical definition, there are two differences: (i) whereas a channel (a, b, p, q) is completely determined by its constituent values, due to the nature of metamodels a *Channel* has its own identity (and so conceivably there could be two *Channels* with the same 4-tuple of values), which can not occur in the mathematical set up in Definition 1; (ii) the function Tok_0 has been combined with *Channel*. This removes some of the modularity of the mathematical model, at the benefit of simplicity.

Model Creation. In our framework, SDF models are created in steps 1 and 2 of Fig. 1. The starting point is an SDF graph created using the well-known open-source SDF[3] tool [21] (step 1). This tool produces output in the form of an XML document, adhering to its own schema (fixed in an XSD). To bring such documents into our framework, we have defined an SDF[3]-*to-SDF Transformation* which produces models conforming to the SDF metamodel of Fig. 3. The transformation definition involves a systematic mapping of the SDF[3] concepts to our SDF metamodel concepts.

4.2   Platform Application Models

A Platform Application Model (PAM) models the multi-processor platform to which the application, modeled as an SDF graph, is mapped. Our PAMs support several features, including (1) heterogeneity, i.e., there can be multiple processors with different types, (2) a partitioning of the processors in voltage/frequency islands, (3) frequency levels each processor can run on, (4) power consumed by a processor at a certain frequency, both when in use and when idle, and (5) power overhead required to switch between frequency levels.

Definition and Metamodel

Definition 2. *Given an SDF graph* $G = (A, D, \mathsf{Tok}_0)$ *with a set of actors* A, *a platform application model (PAM) is a tuple* $\mathcal{P} = (\Pi, \zeta, F, P_{idle}, P_{occ}, P_{tr}, \tau_{act})$ *consisting of*

- *a finite set of processors* $\Pi = \{\pi_1, \ldots, \pi_n\}$. *We assume that* Π *is partitioned into disjoint blocks of voltage/frequency islands (VFIs) such that* $\bigcup \Pi_i = \Pi$, *and* $\Pi_i \cap \Pi_j = \emptyset$ *for* $i \neq j$,
- *a function* $\zeta : \Pi \to 2^A$ *indicating which processors can handle which actors,*
- *a finite set* $F = \{f_1, \ldots, f_m\}$ *of discrete frequencies available to all processors,*
- *a function* $P_{occ} : \Pi \times F \to \mathbb{N}$ *denoting the power consumption (static plus dynamic) of a processor operating at a certain frequency* $f \in F$ *in the operating state,*
- *a function* $P_{idle} : \Pi \times F \to \mathbb{N}$ *denoting the power consumption (static) of a processor operating at a certain frequency* $f \in F$ *in the idle state,*
- *a partial function* $P_{tr} : \Pi \times F^2 \nrightarrow \mathbb{N}$ *denoting the transition overhead between frequencies for each processor* $\pi \in \Pi$, *and*
- *a function* $\tau_{act} : A \times F \to \mathbb{N}_{\geq 1}$ *denoting the actual execution time of each actor (in* A) *mapped to a processor at a certain frequency level (in* F).

Example 2. Exynos 4210 is a state-of-the-art processor used in high-end platforms such as Samsung Galaxy Note, SII, etc. Table 1 shows three frequencies (MHz) $\{f_1, f_2, f_3\} \in F$ [17] and corresponding experimental power consumption. We assume that our PAM contains four Exynos 4210 processors, i.e., $\Pi = \{\pi_1, \pi_2, \pi_3, \pi_4\}$. The processors are partitioned into 2 VFIs, i.e., $\Pi_1 = \{\pi_1, \pi_2\}$ and $\Pi_2 = \{\pi_3, \pi_4\}$. We assume that the power overhead (W) of all $\pi \in \Pi$ is, $P_{tr}(\pi, f_1, f_2) = P_{tr}(\pi, f_2, f_3) = 0.2$ and $P_{tr}(\pi, f_3, f_2) = P_{tr}(\pi, f_2, f_1) = 0.1$.

Table 1. Example platform description

No.	Frequency (MHz)	P_{idle} (W)	P_{occ} (W)
1	1400	0.4	4.6
2	1222	0.3	3.2
3	1033	0.1	1.8

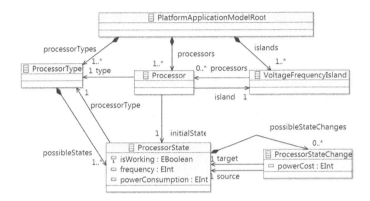

Fig. 4. PAM metamodel

The *PAM Metamodel* capturing most of the concepts of Definition 2 is shown in Fig. 4. A brief explanation can be given as follows:

– *PlatformApplicationModelRoot* stands for the PAM as a whole.
– *ProcessorType* collects the characteristics of a set of processors. In the metamodel, the power and frequency characteristics of a processor are associated with its *type*, creating a reusable layer of indirection with respect to the mathematical model.
– *Processor* stands for the elements of Π. Each *Processor* has a *type* association to the corresponding *ProcessorType*.
– *VoltageFrequencyIsland* stands for the clusters Π_i in the VFI partitioning of Π. The element-of relationship between a processor and its VFI is captured by the (opposite) *island* and *processors* associations.
– *ProcessorState* associates the working/idle state of a processor (type) (the boolean *isWorking* attribute), combined with a *frequency* level, to a *power-Consumption* value. This encodes the P_{occ} and P_{idle} functions of the mathematical definition.
– *ProcessorStateChange* encodes the P_{tr} function of the definition: each instance associates a *powerCost* with a certain pair of *source* and *target Processor-States*.

In a major change with respect to the mathematical definition, we have chosen not to include the ζ and τ_{act} functions in the PAM, but to isolate them in a separate allocation model. This enhances the modularity of the modeling

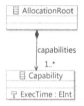

Fig. 5. Allocation metamodel. *Capability* refers to *Actor* in the SDF metamodel and *ProcessorState* in the PAM metamodel.

framework. Apart from this change, all elements of Definition 2 are clearly recognizable in the metamodel, though sometimes encoded in a different manner. In particular, we have introduced the processor types as an intermediate level to enhance modularity; P_{occ} and P_{idle} are combined in *ProcessorState*; and P_{tr} is encoded as *ProcessorStateChange*.

Model Creation. The creation of PAMs corresponds to step 3 in Fig. 1. Although EMF provides a default tree-based model editor, we have built PAM Visual Editor, a domain-specific visual editor for PAMs, by benefiting from state-of-the-art MDE techniques. To build PAM Visual Editor, we have used EuGE-Nia, which can automatically generate a visual editor from an annotated ECore metamodel. We show an example PAM created using this visual editor in Sect. 5.

4.3   Allocation Models

In a heterogeneous system, the freedom of assigning actors $a \in A$ to processors $\pi \in \Pi$ is constrained by which processors can be utilized to execute a particular actor. Thus, in order to run an SDF model on a PAM, we need to know (1) which SDF actors can be run on which processors of the PAM and (2) what their execution times are at given frequencies. This information is encoded in an allocation model, which relates both the SDF and PAM models. Allocation models conform to *Allocation Metamodel* that we define to represent this concern.

The information related to allocation concern is a part of Definition 2, but we have chosen to define it as a separate *Allocation Metamodel* for the sake of modularity to make the PAM metamodel independent of the SDF metamodel.

Definition and Metamodel. The information to be represented in the Allocation metamodel consists of the ζ and τ_{act} functions of Definition 2. The *Allocation Metamodel* is shown in Fig. 5. It contains:

- *AllocationRoot*, which stands for the combined allocation functions ζ and τ_{act} of Definition 2.
- *Capability*, following $\tau_{act} : A \times F \to \mathbb{N}_{\geq 1}$ in Definition 2, refers to *Actor* in the SDF metamodel, and *ProcessorState* (defining the frequency of the processor)

in the PAM metamodel, and yields the time needed to execute the actor at the processor state. At the same time, *ProcessorState* also encodes which processor type an actor can be executed on.

The metamodel is in fact more expressive than the mathematical definition: for instance, the execution time of an actor is not constrained to be always the same for a given frequency level; instead, it may also depend on the processor type.

Model Creation. The creation of Allocation models corresponds to step 4 in Fig. 1. It is supported out-of-the-box via the default tree-based model editor provided by EMF.

4.4 Common Metamodel

In addition to those discussed above, Fig. 1 also shows an element called *Common Metamodel*. This demonstrates an MDE technique for reuse: this metamodel defines the general concept of *Identifiable*, which has a string-valued *identifier* attribute; *Actors* and *ProcessorTypes* are subtypes of *Identifiable* and thereby inherit this feature. Whenever (during extension of the framework) additional reusable concepts are introduced, these can be added to the common metamodel.

4.5 Priced Timed-Automata Models

As mentioned earlier, we use priced timed-automata for energy optimization. Once the SDF, PAM and allocation models are available, one can generate the priced timed-automata model using the *Co-Design-to-*UPPAAL *Transformation* and successive model-to-text transformation. These correspond to steps 5 and 6 in Fig. 1. In Step 7 in Fig. 1, the energy-optimal schedule of an SDF graph can be generated. The ideas in [2] related to how the entities in SDF, PAM and allocation models can be mapped to priced timed-automata models and how the energy-optimal schedule can be calculated are reused in steps 5 and 7.

5 Case Study and Evaluation

In this section, we show the effectiveness of our framework for HW-SW co-design by applying it on a case study. We also demonstrate how our framework satisfies the features stated in Sect. 1, namely: (1) modularity, (2) extensibility, and (3) interoperability. We also evaluate the timing performance of our framework with the help of some other case studies.

5.1 Case Study

As a case study, we consider the dataflow application of the Viola-Jones face detector in Example 1 mapped to a platform with 4 processors of the type Exynos 4210 in Example 2.

Fig. 6. Energy-optimal schedule on four Exynos 4210 processors. The white, red, and green blocks denote the frequencies f_1, f_2, and f_3 respectively. (Color figure online)

Following step 1 in Fig. 1, we have created the SDF graph of the Viola-Jones face detection using SDF³. This SDF graph was already given in Fig. 2. In step 2, we apply SDF³-to-SDF transformation to generate the SDF model conforming to our metamodel for the SDF graph.

In step 3, we create the PAM using the visual editor, as described in Sect. 4.2. The details of this PAM can be found in our technical report [3].

After we have the PAM and SDF models, we create the allocation model that assigns the actors to the processor states with their execution times in step 4.

Once we have the SDF, PAM, and allocation models, we apply the Co-Design-to-UPPAAL transformation in step 5 and the model-to-text transformation in step 6 to generate the priced-timed-automata model that is compatible with UPPAAL CORA. In step 7, we follow the approach presented in [2] to compute the energy-optimal schedule for some given throughput requirements. Figure 6 shows the energy-optimal schedule, for the time per graph iteration constraint of 650 ms for our example. The schedule shows the execution order of the actors at the specific frequency and processors.

5.2   Evaluation

(a) Modularity: To show the modularity of our framework with a concrete example, let us consider the following scenario: We want to analyze the energy consumption of the face detection application on a different hardware platform, viz., Intel Core2 Duo E6850.

Table 2 shows the frequencies and corresponding power consumption of this new proces-

Table 2. Platform description

No.	Freq.	P_{idle}	P_{occ}
1	3006	0.4	55
2	2338	0.3	34
3	1776	0.1	22

sor [17]. For this scenario, we only change the processor type while keeping the number of processors and VFI distributions the same. Now, all we have to do is to develop a new PAM corresponding to this new platform specification and generate the corresponding priced timed-automata model. We reuse the existing SDF model of the application without making any modifications. Using the framework, we derive the energy-optimal schedule shown in Fig. 7 on the new hardware platform, for time per graph iteration constraint of 650 ms.

π1	idle						haar_scal	idle
π2	idle						haar_scal	idle
π3	idle						haar_scal	idle
π4	idle	im_read	dupl_im	integral	haar_det	haar_scal x 22	haar_scal	col_obj	grp_rect

time

Fig. 7. Energy-optimal schedule on four Intel Core 2 Duo E6850 processors

(b) Extensibility: One can extend the framework using the following mechanisms: introducing new models with related metamodels and new transformations; extending existing transformations or metamodels.

As an example, suppose we want to extend our platform models with the concept of "battery". The current version of the platform assumes energy source to be ideal such that the system never runs out of energy. However, we want to include batteries in our HW-SW co-design as resources. This extension can be achieved through the following steps:

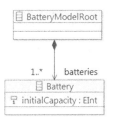

Fig. 8. Battery metamodel

1. Adding a metamodel for batteries: An example battery metamodel is shown in Fig. 8. This metamodel defines the number of batteries in the system with their initial capacities (Coulomb).

*2. Extending the Co-Design-to-*UPPAAL *model transformation:* In order to include the battery model in the scheduling analysis, we have to transform the concepts in the battery metamodel to the concepts in the priced timed-automata domain. This is achieved through extending the Co-Design-to-UPPAAL model transformation in step 5. The extension to the transformation will create the dependency of the processors on the batteries, in such a way that the processors consume charge from these batteries. The extension will further generate separate templates for battery and battery scheduler. The template of the battery keeps track of the current charge. When the battery gets empty, it informs the battery scheduler via synchronization. In that case, the battery scheduler template activates the next available battery. When all batteries are out-of-charge, the processors cannot run anymore. We can extend the Co-Design-to-UPPAAL model transformation without modifying it since ETL allows to extend and reuse transformation modules. Please note that the model-to-text transformation in step 6 stay unaffected by this extension.

(c) Interoperability: In our framework, we utilize SDF[3] for creating SDF graphs and UPPAAL CORA for deriving energy-optimal schedule. To automatically generate UPPAAL CORA models from SDF[3] models, we have implemented model transformations in our framework, thus providing interoperability.

5.3   Timing Performance

To determine the timing performance of our framework, we consider five real-life case studies namely, a Viola-Jones face detector in Fig. 2, a MPEG-4 Decoder [22], an Audio Echo Canceller [11], an MP3 Decoder [20], and an MP3 playback application [25]. We also used an artificial bipartite SDF graph [8] with 4 actors. We assume that these case studies are mapped on Exynos 4210 processors having two frequencies.

We examine the timing performance of our framework in two parts: the first part is the timing performance of our framework, i.e., cumulative computation time of steps 2 (SDF^3-to-SDF transformation), 5 and 6 (Co-Design-to-UPPAAL and model-to-text transformations). The second part is the timing performance of obtaining the optimal schedule via UPPAAL CORA model checker, i.e., step 7.

The case studies show that the time step 2, 5 and 6 take in total increase insignificantly as the number of available processor increases. This is due to the slight increase in the model size with the addition of processors. For step 7, the time required to complete increases exponentially as the number of processor increases, which is because of the fact that the size of the state-space created by the model checker increases exponentially with the size of the model itself.

The details of these case studies can be found in our technical report [3].

6   Conclusions and Future Work

In this paper, we have presented a model-driven framework for HW-SW co-design of dataflow applications. In our framework, we have proposed a reusable set of three coherent metamodels for HW-SW co-design domain. To provide interoperability among domains, we have defined a reusable set of extensible model transformations. We have demonstrated that our framework satisfies the modularity, extensibility and interoperability requirements with a case study.

As future direction of our work, we plan to extend our framework with other analysis techniques such as simulation and automated HW-SW partitioning. We also plan to add code generation functionality to our framework.

Acknowledgements. This research is funded by the EU FP7 project SENSATION (318490) and NWO project BEATS (612.001.303). The authors are grateful to Kim Sunesen from Recore Systems B.V. for providing the case study.

References

1. Software Engineering Group, University of Paderborn. https://www.hni.uni-paderborn.de/en/software-engineering/. Accessed 14 Jan 2016
2. Ahmad, W., Hölzenspies, P.K.F., Stoelinga, M.I.A., van de Pol, J.: Green computing: power optimisation of VFI-based real-time multiprocessor dataflow applications. In: DSD 2015, pp. 271–275, August 2015
3. Ahmad, W., Yildiz, B.M., Rensink, A., Stoelinga, M.: A model-driven framework for hardware-software co-design of dataflow applications. Technical report TR-CTIT-16-09, University of Twente (2016)

4. Basten, T., Hamberg, R., Reckers, F., Verriet, J.: Model-Based Design of Adaptive Embedded Systems. Springer Publishing Company, New York (2013)
5. Behrmann, G., Larsen, K.G., Rasmussen, J.I.: Optimal scheduling using priced timed automata. SIGMETRICS Perform. Eval. Rev. **32**(4), 34–40 (2005)
6. Bondé, L., Dumoulin, C., Dekeyser, J.-L.: Metamodels and MDA transformations for embedded systems. In: Boulet, P. (ed.) Advances in Design and Specification Languages for SoCs, pp. 89–105. Springer, New York (2005)
7. da Silva, A.R.: Model-driven engineering: a survey supported by the unified conceptual model. Comput. Lang. Syst. Struct. **43**, 139–155 (2015)
8. Geilen, M., Basten, T., Stuijk, E.: Minimising buffer requirements of synchronous dataflow graphs with model checking. In: DAC 2005, pp. 819–824 (2005)
9. Gray, I., Matragkas, N., Audsley, N., Indrusiak, L., Kolovos, D., Paige, R.: Model-based hardware generation and programming - the MADES approach. In: ISORCW 2011, pp. 88–96, March 2011
10. Grüttner, K., Hartmann, P.A., Hylla, K., Rosinger, S., Nebel, W., Herrera, F., Villar, E., Brandolese, C., Fornaciari, W., Palermo, G., Ykman-Couvreur, C., Quaglia, D., Ferrero, F., Valencia, R.: The COMPLEX reference framework for HW/SW co-design and power management supporting platform-based design-space exploration. Microprocess. Microsyst. Embed. Hardw. Des. **37**, 966–980 (2013)
11. Hausmans, J.P., Geuns, S.J., Wiggers, M.H., Bekooij, M.J.: Compositional temporal analysis model for incremental hard real-time system design. In: EMSOFT 2012, pp. 185–194 (2012)
12. Herber, P., Glesner, S.: A HW/SW co-verification framework for SystemC. ACM TECS **12**(1s), 61:1–61:23 (2013)
13. Kolovos, D.S., Paige, R.F., Polack, F.A.C.: The epsilon transformation language. In: Vallecillo, A., Gray, J., Pierantonio, A. (eds.) ICMT 2008. LNCS, vol. 5063, pp. 46–60. Springer, Heidelberg (2008). doi:10.1007/978-3-540-69927-9_4
14. Kolovos, D.S., Rose, L.M., Paige, R.F., Polack, F.A.C.: Raising the level of abstraction in the development of GMF-based graphical model editors. In: MISE 2009, pp. 13–19 (2009)
15. Lee, E.A.: Embedded software. Adv. Comput. **56**, 56–97 (2002). http://www.sciencedirect.com/science/article/pii/S0065245802800043
16. Lee, E.A., Messerschmitt, D.G.: Synchronous data flow: describing signal processing algorithm for parallel computation. In: COMPCON 1987, pp. 310–315 (1987)
17. Park, S., Park, J., Shin, D., Wang, Y., Xie, Q., Pedram, M., Chang, N.: Accurate modeling of the delay and energy overhead of dynamic voltage and frequency scaling in modern microprocessors. IEEE Trans. Comput Aided Des. Integr. Circuits Syst. (TCAD) **32**(5), 695–708 (2013)
18. Sprinkle, J., Rumpe, B., Vangheluwe, H., Karsai, G.: Metamodelling. In: Giese, H., Karsai, G., Lee, E., Rumpe, B., Schätz, B. (eds.) MBEERTS 2007. LNCS, vol. 6100, pp. 57–76. Springer, Heidelberg (2010). doi:10.1007/978-3-642-16277-0_3
19. Steinberg, D., Budinsky, F., Merks, E., Paternostro, M.: EMF: Eclipse Modeling Framework. Pearson Education, Boston (2008)
20. Stuijk, S.: Predictable mapping of streaming applications on multiprocessors. Ph.D. thesis (2007)
21. Stuijk, S., Geilen, M., Basten, T.: SDF³: SDF for free. In: ACSD 2006, pp. 276–278, June 2006
22. Theelen, B., Geilen, M.C.W., Basten, T., Voeten, J.P.M., Gheorghita, S.V., Stuijk, S.: A scenario-aware data flow model for combined long-run average and worst-case performance analysis. In: MEMOCODE 2006, pp. 185–194 (2006)

23. Viola, P., Jones, M.: Rapid object detection using a boosted cascade of simple features. In: CVPR 2001, vol. 1, pp. I-511–I-518 (2001)
24. Völter, M., Stahl, T., Bettin, J., Haase, A., Helsen, S.: Model-Driven Software Development: Technology, Engineering, Management. John Wiley & Sons (2013)
25. Wiggers, M.H.. Aperiodic multiprocessor scheduling for real-time stream processing applications. Ph.D. thesis (2009)

Symbolic Analysis of Hybrid Systems Involving Numerous Discrete Changes Using Loop Detection

Kenichi Betsuno$^{(\boxtimes)}$, Shota Matsumoto, and Kazunori Ueda

Department of Computer Science and Engineering, Waseda University,
3-4-1, Okubo, Shinjuku-ku, Tokyo 169-8555, Japan
{betsuno,matsusho,ueda}@ueda.info.waseda.ac.jp

Abstract. Hybrid systems are dynamical systems that include both continuous and discrete changes. Some hybrid systems involve a large or infinite number of discrete changes within an infinitesimal-width region of phase space. Systems with sliding mode are typical examples of such hybrid systems. It is difficult to analyze such hybrid systems through ordinary numerical simulation, since the time required for simulation increases in proportion to the number of discrete changes. In this paper, we propose a method to symbolically analyze such models involving numerous discrete changes by detecting loops and checking loop invariants of the model's behavior. The method handles parameterized hybrid systems and checks inclusion of parameterized states focusing on the values of a switching function that dominate the dynamics of sliding mode. We implemented the main part of the method in our symbolic hybrid system simulator HyLaGI, and conducted analysis of example models.

Keywords: Hybrid systems · Sliding mode · Loop invariants · Verification · Symbolic analysis

1 Introduction

Hybrid systems [6] are dynamical systems which include both continuous and discrete changes. This feature enables a number of problems in a variety of fields to be modeled as hybrid systems, e.g., physics, control engineering, and biology. Examples of hybrid systems include physical systems with impact and electronic circuits with switching. In these systems, impact and switching are expressed as discrete changes. Many of cyber-physical systems are also regarded as hybrid systems, which include discrete decisions by computational parts and hybrid behavior of physical parts. Some hybrid systems include numerous discrete changes such as infinitely frequent switching. Such systems are difficult to simulate due to the explosion in the number of discrete changes, as the processing of discrete changes is the most costly part of simulation except for systems with

---

This paper is an extended version of our earlier article [2].

© Springer International Publishing AG 2017
C. Berger et al. (Eds.): CyPhy 2016, LNCS 10107, pp. 17–30, 2017.
DOI: 10.1007/978-3-319-51738-4_2

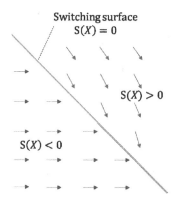

Fig. 1. Gradient vectors in the sliding mode

complex continuous dynamics. In this paper, we propose a method to analyze such models involving numerous discrete changes by detecting looping behavior of the models.

1.1 Sliding Mode

Sliding mode control is one of the control methods which switches the continuous dynamics of the systems when the system comes across a predefined surface, which is called a switching surface. In the sliding mode, the directions of the gradient vectors of the system (Fig. 1) are towards the switching surface $S(X)$ = 0 on the both sides of the surface. As a result, the behavior of the system is bound to the surface as if it is sliding on the surface, which is the reason why it is called a sliding mode. Systems with sliding modes can be regarded as hybrid systems involving infinitely frequent discrete changes of its control input. Such control cannot be performed in real systems as the switching of control inputs cannot be done within zero time. To reflect this, we regard the switching surface not as a simple boundary but as an infinitesimal band. This band is called a sliding region, in which the trajectory of the sliding mode is confined. Each switching function is defined as $S1(X) = S(X)$ and $S2(X) = S(X)+ \epsilon$, where $S(X)$ is the ideal switching function and $\epsilon > 0$ is infinitesimal (see Fig. 2). In this paper, we define a sliding mode as a behavior along a *sliding region*, a region enclosed by $S1(X)$ and $S2(X)$.

Example: Brake Control with Sliding Mode Control. In this paper, we use a brake control problem as a running example, whose objective is to stop a vehicle at a target position. In this model, two control inputs are available: applying the brake or not. The position of the vehicle is denoted by variable x. The switching function is $S(x, x') = x + x' - 100$, where x' denotes the time derivative dx/dt. Introducing a switching function $S(x, x')$, the function of the current position x and the velocity x', these two control inputs are switched

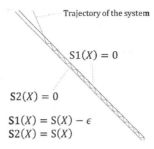

Fig. 2. Behavior in the sliding mode considering the switching time

according to whether the value of the switching function is positive or negative. The example model is given in the form of a HydLa [10] program. HydLa is a constraint-based language for modeling hybrid systems, and its detailed syntax and semantics are found in [10].

Figure 3 shows the example model. The top nine lines are definitions of constraints. In HydLa, all values of variables are functions of time, and each constraint is enabled at the initial time of the model. The constraint INIT describes the initial state of the model. The value of x' is given by the inequality 0 < x' < 80, which means the initial velocity is uncertain but has a fixed range. The variable sw dominates the continuous behavior of the vehicle (see ACC). EPS describes the width of the sliding region denoted by eps. The temporal operator [] means that the constraint always holds from the time point at which the constraint is enabled. S defines the switching surfaces denoted by s1 and s2 that enclose the sliding region. In this paper, we use variables s1 and s2 to represent the values of $S1(X)$ and $S2(X)$ at each time point, which are called *switching variables*. SW_CONST, SW_ON and SW_OFF describe the behavior of sw, which is constant by default and switches only when the vehicle comes across the switching surface. The postfix minus sign in sw- denotes the left-hand limit $\lim_{t_l \uparrow t} sw(t_l)$. ACC describes the acceleration of the vehicle and depends on the value of sw. STOP stops the vehicle if the speed equals zero and prevents the vehicle from moving back. The bottom line describes the priorities between the constraints using << in the form of a partial order. SW_ON and SW_OFF are stronger than SW_CONST, and STOP is stronger than ACC, both because they describe an exceptional behavior of the vehicle.

Figure 4 shows one of the trajectories of the model assuming that the value of eps is sufficiently small so that $S1(X)$, $S2(X)$ and $S(X)$ can be regarded as the same. The description of the states indicated as (1)–(7) in Fig. 4 are as follows:

1. The system is in its initial state.
2. The vehicle doesn't apply the brake and moves at a constant speed because S < 0.
3. The system reaches the switching surface and switches the control input; the vehicle begins to apply the brake.

```
INIT <=> x = 0 /\ 0 < x' < 80 /\ sw = 0.
EPS <=> 0 < eps < 0.1 /\ [](eps' = 0).
S <=> [](s1 = x' + x - 100 - eps /\
         s2 = x' + x - 100).
SW_CONST <=> [](sw' = 0).
SW_ON  <=> [](s1- = 0 /\ s1'- >= 0 => sw = 1 - sw-).
SW_OFF <=> [](s2- = 0 /\ s2'- <= 0 => sw = 1 - sw-).
ACC <=> [](x'' = -50 * sw).
STOP <=> [](x' = 0 => x'' = 0).

INIT, SW_CONST << (SW_ON, SW_OFF), ACC << STOP, S, EPS.
```

Fig. 3. HydLa program of the vehicle with sliding mode control

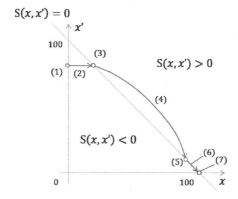

Fig. 4. Trajectory of the vehicle with sliding mode control

4. The vehicle moves at a constant acceleration because of the brake.
5. The system reaches the switching ssurface again and switches the control input.
6. The system enters the sliding mode, that is, moves along the sliding surface.
7. The vehicle stops at the destination $x = 10ss0$.

2 Proposed Method

The goal of our method is rigorous simulation and reasoning of hybrid systems which include sliding modes and other chattering behaviors. In this paper, we focus on the central part of our method, namely how to establish conditions that should hold upon exit of sliding mode, which will then enable us to continue simulation beyond the sliding mode if desired. This involves the recognition and analysis of a looping behavior with an arbitrary large number of iterations. Since fully automatic analysis of loops is hard in general, we allows some auxiliary information to be provided for the analysis. Specifically, the input and output of our method, up until (but not beyond) loop analysis, are as follows:

Input:

1. Model description given as a HydLa program that expresses a target system,
2. Model specification given as a proposition that should be satisfied by the system upon exit of a loop,
3. Termination condition under which the system definitely exits from the loop,
4. Switching function which the switching of the dynamics depends on.

Output: Whether the system will satisfy the model specification or not upon exit of the loop.

The key idea of the method is to regard the sliding mode as a loop, and the occurrence of the sliding mode will be detected through loop detection. The overall flow of the method is shown in Fig. 5. The proposed method consists of the following four steps:

1. **loop detection:** detecting a loop which may be sliding mode
2. **establishing loop invariant:** verifying that the system stays in the sliding region during the loop
3. **termination check:** verifying that the system will exit from the loop
4. **deducing model specification:** confirming that the system satisfies the goal conditions if it was within the sliding region and satisfies the loop termination condition.

2.1 Loop Detection

In this step, we judge whether newly computed continuous behaviours have already been computed in the past. A set of continuous behaviors is expressed by parameterized functions of time that are computed by symbolic simulation. Continuous behaviors contain information about initial values of state variables and constraints imposed on state variables. If the new behaviors are found to be already computed, it means that the behaviors of the system enter a loop and all the values of variables stay in an already computed range. In our previous work [12], we proposed a method to detect such loops focusing on inclusion relation between continuous behaviors. However, the method required the behaviors of *all* variables in the system to be included, which is not the case with many practical systems including sliding mode control. To solve this problem, we propose a new inclusion relation focusing only on switching variables as follows:

Definition 1. *Continuous behavior* β_1 *includes continuous behavior* β_2 *about switching functions if*

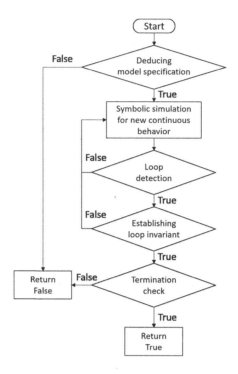

Fig. 5. Flowchart of the proposed method with a symbolic simulator

1. *The constraints imposed on the state variables are the same.*
2. *The parameterized values of $S1(X)$ and $S2(X)$ at the beginning of β_2 are included in those of β_1.*
3. *The parameterized values of the n-th derivatives of $S1(X)$ and $S2(X)$ at the beginning of β_2 are included in those of β_1, where n is any positive integer.*

The inclusion relation between two parameterized values means that a domain of one parameterized value includes that of the other. For example, provided that a parameter p satisfies $p \in [0, 1]$ where $[a, b]$ denotes a closed interval, $p \times 0.8 \subseteq p$ holds. If the above conditions are satisfied, we can conclude that the system enters a loop about switching variables and that the value of each switching variable stays in a computed range.

We chose HydLa as a modeling language that does not come with an explicit notion of loops, while hybrid automata [4] represent explicit state transition. However, even if we choose hybrid automata, loop detection described here is still necessary because loops expressed by hybrid automata just represent those of control flow, while we are concerned with loops defined as state inclusion.

2.2   Establishing Loop Invariant

In this step, we verify that the loop detected in the previous step satisfies the loop invariant, which means that the systems stay in the sliding region. To verify that, we must confirm that the condition $S1(X) \leq 0 \leq S2(X)$ holds throughout the first iteration of the loop. If it does, we can conclude that the condition holds until the loop terminates, because the values of switching variables $S1(X)$ and $S2(X)$ stay within the range of the first iteration as described in Sect. 2.1. Assuming that we can obtain information about the trajectories of switching variables from the symbolic simulator, this step is conducted by checking those trajectories for one iteration.

2.3   Termination Check

In this step, we verify that the termination condition eventually holds. We can verify it by finding some $F(X)$ and a target value g that satisfies the conditions below:

– The value of $F(X)$ increases at least by some $k \in \mathbb{R}_+$ in each iteration.
– $F(X) \geq g \wedge LoopInvariant(X) \Rightarrow LoopTerminationCondition(X)$ is valid.

Note that similar conditions are found in the proof of loop termination in programming languages, and $F(X)$ acts as a loop variant. In the second condition, we can also adopt an equality $F(X) = g$ instead of $F(X) \geq g$ if $F(X)$ is known to be continuous. The choice about which one should be used depends on the form of $LoopTerminationCondition(X)$.

Example 1. In the brake control example, we define $F(X) := -x'$ and $g := 0$. It should be verified that $\exists k \in \mathbb{R}_+ (\forall i \in \mathbb{N} (F_{i+1} - F_i \geq k))$. In the loop, the vehicle repeats braking and moving at a constant speed. Provided that the system is in the first quadrant of the phase space, braking causes the system to move in the positive direction of the x axis and the negative direction of the x' axis (see Fig. 1). Thus, x' decreases at least by $\epsilon(\mathbf{eps})$ in each braking, which means $\forall i \in \mathbb{N}(F_{i+1} - F_i \geq \epsilon)$.

2.4   Deducing Model Specification

In this step, it is confirmed that the system meets the target specification if it stays inside of the sliding region and satisfies the loop termination condition. Thus, the validity of the following formula should be verified:

$$LoopInvariant(X) \wedge LoopTerminationCondition(X) \Rightarrow \\ TargetSpecification(X) \tag{1}$$

Note that the concrete form of $LoopInvariant(X)$ here is the inequality $S1(X) \leq 0 \leq S2(X)$. The verification of Formula (1) can be performed statically, and this is why it is performed at the beginning rather than the end of the analysis in Fig. 5.

Table 1. Case branching in the brake control model with SMC

Initial speed x'	Existence of a loop
$(0, 50 - 35\sqrt{2})$	No
$50 - 35\sqrt{2}$	No
$(50 - 35\sqrt{2}, 80)$	Yes

Example 2. In the brake control example, *LoopInvariant(X)* is $x + x' - 100 - \epsilon \le 0 \le x + x' - 100$, *LoopTerminationCondition*(X) is $x' = 0$, and *TargetSpecification*(X) is $100 - \epsilon \le x \le 100 \wedge x' = 0$. We can transform *LoopInvariant(X)* into $100 - \epsilon \le x \le 100$ by letting $x' = 0$. Here, $100 - \epsilon \le x \le 100 \wedge x' = 0$ is exactly the same as *TargetSpecification(X)*, therefore Formula (1) is verified.

3 Experiment

We have implemented the loop detection step in HyLaGI [7], which is a simulator of HydLa programs that we have developed. HyLaGI has several key features below:

- HyLaGI performs all computations symbolically and the result is free from computation errors caused by floating-point arithmetic.
- Uncertain values in systems are expressed by symbolic parameters. This enables parameter analysis of models.
- Case analysis is conducted on demand if the uncertainty of the systems leads to qualitative branching of behavior, e.g., whether two balls collide or not.

With this implementation, we conducted experiments of loop detection for several models. In this section, we also discuss how the remaining properties can be derived from the output of HyLaGI.

Brake Control Model with Sliding Mode Control. The first example is the brake control model with sliding mode control, which is described in Sect. 1.1. In order to detect a loop of the model, the initial speed of the vehicle should be a parameterized value such as $p \in (0, 80)$. As for eps, we use a small fixed value 0.5. If we use an uncertain value for eps, the current symbolic computation engine fails to judge an inclusion relation of continuous behaviors, while it can still simulate up to the second braking. Even if we adopt a fixed value as eps, the proposed method has an advantage in reducing computational costs of simulation. With this initial condition, the computation with our implementation branched into three different cases depending on the initial speed, as shown in Table 1.

When $0 < x' \le 50 - 35\sqrt{2}$, the vehicle stops on the first braking and the system doesn't enter a loop. Otherwise, the implementation detected a loop because the state of the first braking includes the state of the second braking. The

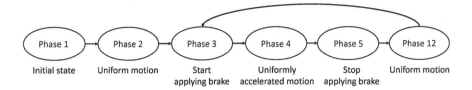

Fig. 6. State transition of the brake control model

parameterized values of $s1$ and its derivatives at the first and second brakings are shown in Table 2, where $p_{s1} \in ((-70\sqrt{2} - 101)/2, -41/2)$. Figure 6 shows a state transition diagram computed by HyLaGI.

Table 2. The parameterized values of s1 and s1' at the first and second brakings

Variable	First braking	Second braking
$s1$	0	0
$s1'$	$p_{s1} + 201/2$	$50 - \sqrt{10401 + 4p_{s1}(101 + p_{s1})}/2$

In Fig. 6, Phase 1 corresponds to the initial state of the model. After that, the vehicle moves at a constant speed (Phase 2) and applies the brake when $s1 = 0$ (Phase 3). The speed decreases by the brake (Phase 4) and the braking is stopped when $s2 = 0$ (Phase 5). The vehicle moves in uniform motion again (Phase 12) and the state transits back to Phase 3 because the next state of Phase 12 is included by Phase 3. Note that this inclusion can be detected by focusing on switching variables, which is an important difference from the previous work.

In this model, the initial speed is abstracted to an interval value $(0, 80)$. If we adopted some fixed value as the initial speed, the first derivatives of the switching variables would decrease at each braking and no inclusion between states could have been detected. For example, Table 3 shows the values of variables at each time point of braking where the initial speed equals 80. In Table 3, $s1$ and $s2$ and their derivatives are fixed values, and the values of the derivatives at the first braking do not include those at the second braking, which means that the loop detection fails. This is why we need to abstract the initial speed in this model.

For the steps after loop detection, the readers are referred to Sect. 2 for this example.

If we conducted symbolic simulation without loop detection, the size and complexity of the symbolic formulas of state variables would increase quickly, which would make the simulation finally come to a halt.

Optical Fiber Model. The next model is an optical fiber model; a (slow) ray proceeds inside an optical fiber. When the ray hits a boundary, total internal reflection occurs and the ray is confined in the core. In this model, we suppose that the fiber forms a circle and the attenuation of the light can be ignored (Fig. 7). The HydLa program is shown in Fig. 8. The variables x and y denote

Table 3. The values of variables at each braking with $x'(0) = 80$

Variable	First braking	Second braking
$s1$	0	0
$s2$	1/2	1/2
$s1'$	80	$50 - 5\sqrt{38}$
$s2'$	80	$50 - 5\sqrt{38}$
x	41/2	$(101 + 10\sqrt{38})/2$
x'	80	$50 - 5\sqrt{38}$

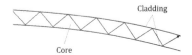
Cladding

Core

Fig. 7. Trajectory of an optical fiber model

```
INIT <=> x = 0 /\ y = r + eps / 2 /\ x' = 1 /\ y' = -1.
CONSTANTS <=> [](r = 5) /\ eps = 0.1 /\ [](eps' = 0).
S <=> [](s1 = x^2 + y^2 - (r+eps)^2 /\ s2 = x^2 + y^2 - r^2).
XCONST <=> [](x'' = 0).
YCONST <=> [](y'' = 0).
REFLECT_1 <=> [](s1- = 0 =>
  x' = x'- - 2*(x'- * x- + y'- * y-) / (r+eps)^2 * x- /\
  y' = y'- - 2*(x'- * x- + y'- * y-) / (r+eps)^2 * y-).
REFLECT_2 <=> [](s2- = 0 =>
  x' = x'- - 2*(x'- * x- + y'- * y-) / r^2 * x- /\
  y' = y'- - 2*(x'- * x- + y'- * y-) / r^2 * y-).

INIT, (XCONST, YCONST) << (REFLECT_1, REFLECT_2) << S, CONSTANTS.
```

Fig. 8. HydLa program of the optical fiber model

the position of the ray, while r denotes the radius of the circle and equals five. The width of the fiber is denoted by eps and is set to 0.1.

In the loop detection of this model, HyLaGI detected a loop between the first reflection on the inner edge and the second one. Table 4 shows the values of state variables at each inner reflection. Here, the symbolic expressions about x, y and their derivatives at the second inner reflection are different from those at the first inner reflection and are more complex. However, s1, s2 and their derivatives are the same and that is the reason why we can conclude that the behavior of the system forms a loop. It follows from this result that the time of each cycle of the loop is constant because the trajectories of s1 and s2 are both constant in the loop.

Table 4. Result of the loop detection experiment of the optical fiber model

Variable	First inner reflection	Second inner reflection
$s1$	$-101/100$	$-101/100$
$s2$	0	0
$s1'$	$-9799^{1/2} \times 1/10$	$-9799^{1/2} \times 1/10$
$s2'$	$-9799^{1/2} \times 1/10$	$-9799^{1/2} \times 1/10$
x	$(101 - 9799^{1/2}) \times 1/40$	$(103937993^{1/2} \times 525301 + 1055803 \times 9799^{1/2}$ $+\, 98393897 - 10607^{1/2} \times 48954599)$ $\times\, 1/2080800000$
x'	$(201 + 101 \times 9799^{1/2})$ $\times\, 1/10000$	$(10141798597 + 103937993^{1/2} \times 2050401$ $+\, 10607^{1/2} \times 5045919499$ $-\, 9799^{1/2} \times 4121103) \times 1/520200000000$
y	$(101 + 9799^{1/2}) \times 1/40$	$(10607^{1/2} \times 48954599 + 103937993^{1/2} \times 525301$ $+\, 98393897 - 9799^{1/2} \times 1055803)$ $\times\, 1/2080800000$
y'	$(101 \times 9799^{1/2} - 201)$ $\times\, 1/10000$	$(10607^{1/2} \times 5045919499 - 10141798597$ $-\, 103937993^{1/2} \times 2050401 - 9799^{1/2}$ $\times\, 4121103) \times 1/520200000000$

Pushing Two Balls. We cite this model from [5]. In the initial state of the model, two balls are touching each other and are not moving. After one second, we push one of the balls toward the other until 3.5 s elapse. While pushing, infinitely frequent collisions between the two balls occur; therefore direct simulation is impossible. To handle such infiniteness, we use our loop detection method. Figure 9 shows a HydLa program of this model. We use an infinitesimal parameter eps as the initial distance between the two balls. The variables x1 and x2 denote the positions of the balls. A timer variable tt is used to trigger events about pushing. The diameter of each ball and the coefficient of restitution are set to one.

The implemented system detected a loop between the first and the second collisions. Table 5 shows the values of variables at each collision. As in the optical fiber model, the values of s1, s2 and their derivatives are the same between two collisions, while x1 and x2 are different.

If we want to confirm that the loop invariant is satisfied, we need to check the validity of the following proposition derived from the symbolic simulation:

$$\forall t \in [0, \sqrt{2eps}] \; (\forall eps \in [0, 0.01] \; (-0.5t(t - \sqrt{2eps}) - eps \leq 0 \tag{2}$$
$$\wedge \; 0 \leq -0.5t(t - \sqrt{2eps})))$$

We can confirm the validity of Formula 2 by the *Reduce* function of Mathematica currently used as the symbolic engine of HyLaGI.

Next, let us consider how to prove loop termination caused by the inequality tt- ≥ 3.5. As shown in Table 5, the values of s1, s2 and their derivatives are

```
INIT <=> x1 = 0 /\ x2 = 1 + eps /\ x1' = 0 /\ x2' = 0.
TIMER <=> tt = 0 /\ [](tt' = 1).
S <=> [](s1 = x2 - x1 - 1 - eps /\ s2 = x2 - x1 - 1).
FORCE(x) <=> [](tt- < 1 => x'' = 0)
   /\ [](1 <= tt- < 3.5 => x'' = 1)
   /\ [](tt- >= 3.5 => x'' = 0).
CONSTV(x) <=> [](x'' = 0).
COLLISION <=> [](s2- = 0 => x1' = x2'- /\ x2' = x1'-).
EPS <=> 0 < eps < 0.01 /\ [](eps' = 0).

INIT, S, EPS, TIMER,
(FORCE(x1), CONSTV(x2)) << COLLISION.
```

Fig. 9. HydLa program of the pushing of two balls

Table 5. The values of variables at each collision

Variable	First collision	Second collision
$s1$	$-eps$	$-eps$
$s2$	0	0
$s1'$	$-\sqrt{2eps}$	$-\sqrt{2eps}$
$s2'$	$-\sqrt{2eps}$	$-\sqrt{2eps}$
$x1$	eps	$5eps$
$x2$	$1+eps$	$1+5eps$
$x1'$	0	$\sqrt{2eps}$
$x2'$	$\sqrt{2eps}$	$2\sqrt{2eps}$
tt	$1+\sqrt{2eps}$	$1+3\sqrt{2eps}$

the same after each collision. In addition, their second derivatives are $s2'' = s1'' = x2'' - x1'' = 1$ throughout the loop. Therefore, the time interval of each iteration is also constant, and from Table 5 we can derive that tt increases by $2\sqrt{2eps}$ at each iteration. Adopting $F(X) :=$ tt and $g := 3.5$, it is obvious that $F(X)$ eventually exceeds g, and the proposition $F(X) \geq g \wedge LoopInvariant(X) \Rightarrow$ tt- ≥ 3.5 also holds obviously.

Finally, consider x2 − x1 − 1 ≤ eps as a target specification, which means that the relative position of the second ball from the first one is less than eps when we stop pushing. This specification is implied from the invariant about s1, that is, s1 = x2 − x1 − 1 − eps ≤ 0. Thus, the specification is verified.

4   Related Work

In previous work, the sliding mode dynamics involving chattering was approximated by non-chattering dynamics on a sliding surface [1,3,8,11]. Most of these approaches adopt numerical simulation methods and aim at simulating such models with approximation. Our approach is based on symbolic simulation and focuses on validated simulation of parameterized hybrid systems rather than simulation with approximations. Compared to those numerical methods, our approach can deal with hybrid models with parameters and need not approximate the behavior of the models. Owing to its symbolic approach, the proposed method is currently applicable only to linear and simple nonlinear models. Challenges for the future include extending this approach to nonlinear models without analytic solutions, which involves integration of symbolic computation and rigorous numerical computation.

A hybrid theorem prover KeYmaera [9] supports verification of parametric hybrid systems. However, KeYmaera aims at verification, while our goal is to perform validated simulation of parametric hybrid systems.

5   Conclusion

In this paper, we proposed a method for the symbolic simulation of hybrid systems with a large or an infinite number of discrete changes, most typically due to sliding mode. We also implemented the algorithm for detecting loops caused by sliding mode by extending HyLaGI, a symbolic simulator of parameterized hybrid systems. Although the automatic discovery of loop invariants and loop variants is our future work, we found that once a loop is detected, the output of HyLaGI provides us with useful information for the rest of the four steps discussed in Sect. 2. Extending our algorithm and implementation with differential invariants and differential variants and continuing symbolic simulation until and beyond the exit of a loop is our future work. This part of verification is strongly dependent on the hardness of each model, since it is necessary to verify that the system will eventually satisfy exit conditions of a loop rather than simulating the system step by step. Automatic discovery of loop invariants and loop variants may be possible for some systems, but in general, interacting with users for auxiliary information as in proof assistant systems seems to be a key idea for the verification of complex models.

We have found that some models need to be abstracted with respect to the initial states. At present, such abstraction is given manually, but it is of course desirable to automate this step using a kind of abstraction refinement procedure that performs both refinement and generalization. Handling models with multiple switching surfaces is another direction of our future work.

References

1. Aljarbouh, A., Caillaud, B.: Chattering-free simulation of hybrid dynamical systems with the Functional Mock-Up Interface 2.0. In: Proceedings of 1st Japanese Modelica Conference, Linköping Electronic Conference Proceedings, vol. 124, no. 013, pp. 95–105 (2016)

2. Betsuno, K., Matsumoto, S., Wakatsuki, Y., Ueda, K.: Analysis of hybrid systems involving numerous discrete changes using loop detection. In: Proceedings of 30th Annual Conference of the Japanese Society for Artificial Intelligence, 1F3-4 (2016). (in Japanese)
3. Filippov, A.F.: Differential Equations with Discontinuous Right-Hand Sides. Mathematics and its Applications. Kluwer Academic, Boston (1988)
4. Henzinger, T.: The theory of hybrid automata. In: Proceedings of LICS 1996, pp. 278–292. IEEE Computer Society Press (1996)
5. Lee, E.A.: Constructive models of discrete and continuous physical phenomena. IEEE Access **2**, 797–821 (2014)
6. Lunze, J.: Handbook of Hybrid Systems Control: Theory, Tools, Applications. Cambridge University Press, Cambridge (2009)
7. Matsumoto, S., Kono, F., Kobayashi, T., Ueda, K.: HyLaGI: symbolic implementation of a hybrid constraint language HydLa. Electron. Notes Theoret. Comput. Sci. **317**, 109–115 (2015)
8. Mosterman, P.J., Zhao, F., Biswas, G.: Sliding mode model semantics and simulation for hybrid systems. In: Antsaklis, P., Lemmon, M., Kohn, W., Nerode, A., Sastry, S. (eds.) HS 1997. LNCS, vol. 1567, pp. 218–237. Springer, Heidelberg (1999). doi:10.1007/3-540-49163-5_12
9. Platzer, A., Quesel, J.-D.: KeYmaera: a hybrid theorem prover for hybrid systems (system description). In: Armando, A., Baumgartner, P., Dowek, G. (eds.) IJCAR 2008. LNCS (LNAI), vol. 5195, pp. 171–178. Springer, Heidelberg (2008). doi:10.1007/978-3-540-71070-7_15
10. Ueda, K., Matsumoto, S., Takeguchi, A., Hosobe, H., Ishii, D.: HydLa: a high-level language for hybrid systems. In: Proceedings of 2nd Workshop on Logics for System Analysis (LfSA 2012, affiliated with CAV 2012), pp. 3–17 (2012)
11. Utkin, V.I.: Sliding Modes in Control and Optimization. Springer, Berlin (1992)
12. Wakatsuki, Y., Matsumoto, S., Ueda, K.: Introduction of LTL model checking to a hybrid constraint system HyLaGI. In: Proceedings of 30th Annual Conference of the Japanese Society for Artificial Intelligence, 1F3-1 (2016). (in Japanese)

SysML to NuSMV Model Transformation via Object-Orientation

Georgiana Caltais[1]([⊠]), Florian Leitner-Fischer[2], Stefan Leue[1],
and Jannis Weiser[1]

[1] Department for Computer and Information Science,
University of Konstanz, Konstanz, Germany
`{Georgiana.Caltais,Stefan.Leue,Jannis.Weiser}@uni-konstanz.de`
[2] ZF Friedrichshafen AG, Active and Passive Safety Technology,
Friedrichshafen, Germany
`florian.leitner-fischer@zf.com`

Abstract. This paper proposes a transformation of SysML models into
the NuSMV input language. The transformation is performed automatically using SysMV-Ja and relies on a notion of intermediate model structuring the relevant SysML components in an object-oriented fashion.

1 Introduction

The complexity and size of safety-critical systems is steadily growing as technology advances. Hence, (semi-) formal approaches to the design, modelling and
reasoning on the correctness of such systems plays a very important rôle. Nevertheless, introducing "friendly" formal frameworks into industrial settings is not
at all a trivial task.

The OMG System Modelling Language (SysML) [14,17,25] is a graphical
modelling language fairly intuitive and easy to learn by software engineers.
SysML has been successfully used in practice. Nevertheless, the application of
rigorous verification techniques such as model-checking on SysML-based inputs
is usually not something that engineers are keen or trained to do.

In this paper, we propose a model transformation from SysML block definition diagrams and state machines to the input language of the NuSMV model-
checker [8], implemented in the automated tool SysMV-Ja. Our approach exploits
a SysML intermediate model. The intermediate model provides an object-oriented
view of the SysML modelling concepts relevant for the work in this paper. This
object-oriented approach could be exploited, in the future, to transform SysML
into the languages of other model-checkers, in a structured way.

The intermediate representation is then exploited to guide a 2-step transformation from SysML to NuSMV input, in a structured way. Advantages of
considering such an intermediate model include: the familiarity of developers
with the Object-Oriented Programming-paradigm, the modularity of the approach, and the possibility of tracing back into the model potential sources of
unwanted behaviour, as reported by the model-checker.

© Springer International Publishing AG 2017
C. Berger et al. (Eds.): CyPhy 2016, LNCS 10107, pp. 31–45, 2017.
DOI: 10.1007/978-3-319-51738-4_3

Related work. There is a considerable amount of literature on providing (formal) semantics of SysML/UML, or on automatically translating associated models into inputs for different analysis tools.

The work in [9], for instance, presents a systematic, but direct translation of statecharts to SMV. As the approach is strictly tailored for the input language of SMV, it cannot be easily adapted for other model checkers or verification tools.

Hugo/RT [1] is a tool that translates UML into corresponding input for the Spin [18] model checker, via the so-called UTE intermediate format. UTE is a textual format that most of the engineers and programmers have to become acquainted with, in contrast to the more familiar Object-Oriented Programming-paradigm exploited in our paper. Another approach for verifying UML models using Spin is given in [23]. Even though the translation from UML to Promela–the input language of Spin–is straightforward and thus, little reusable, the automated tool vUML provides intuitive feedback to the user in case an error was found during verification.

In [21], SysML specifications are automatically translated into equivalent behavioural UML models. The latter are further used to derive test cases and executable test scripts, in the context of a model-based testing tool. The main difference with the work in [21] is that we use the Object-Oriented Programming-paradigm in order to model both the static and the dynamic structure of systems. The approach in [21] uses UML Class Diagrams to represent the static structure of systems and UML State Machines to represent their dynamics. Moreover, the unifying framework of object orientation enables us to define stereotypes and facilitates extensions of the standard SysML/UML semantics, if so desired. Nevertheless, our work does not tackle the issue of combining multiple profiles and avoiding specification conflicts. For a contribution along this research direction we refer, for instance, to [13] where some of the challenges of combining SysML and the OMG MARTE profile [15] are addressed.

More theoretical approaches, usually less appealing for engineers and software developers, propose formalisations of SysML/UML as Process Algebras [4,16] and Petri Nets [10,12]. Model checking of hierarchical state machines has been addressed in [3], for instance, where Kripke structures were employed as their formalisation.

A formal intermediate model of UML behavioural diagrams was also proposed in [11], in terms of the so-called Configuration Transition Systems (CTS's). Similarly to our approach, the results in [11] provide a systematic way of generating inputs for the NuSMV model checker based on intermediate models. In [11], the authors also emphasise on the importance of exploiting intermediate models in order to provide useful feedback to the designer. In accordance, the CTS's can be graphically visualised.

Labelled Transition Systems and Structural Operational Semantics [26] were exploited in [27] in order to provide a modular semantics of UML-RT –a dialect of UML that supports the development of hierarchical systems following a component-oriented approach. As for the case of UML-RT, rigorous formalisations are easier to define over textual terms. Such representations, however, are difficult to use and follow in practice. For an attempt to overcome this type of issues, we refer to the results in [19] where the authors present a graphical user interface-based tool that supports a visual language called v-Promela. This language is the graphical extension of Promela, and the v-Promela notation inherits largely from the aforementioned UML-RT notation. Additionally, a semantics of UML-RT in AsmL–an object-oriented software specification language based on the theory of Abstract State Machines–was proposed in [22]. In connection with our current work, the idea of employing a meta-model defining the syntactic structure of the UML-RT modelling concepts was exploited as well. One the one hand, in our context, following the AsmL approach is not necessary as the syntactic structure of SysML/UML models can be expressed by means of Block Definition Diagrams. On the other hand, AsmL is a language that most of the engineers and developers would have to acquire.

The work in [24] is a classical reference on how to implement statecharts in Promela/SPIN using hierarchical automata defined based on operational semantics as intermediate format. A denotational meta-modelling of the semantics of a part of UML suitable for describing and constraining object structures was proposed in [20]. The results in [7] pave the way to a formalisation of UML in terms of the so-called System Models consisting of elements that describe the structure, behaviour and interaction of systems.

These more formal approaches are orthogonal works that go beyond the scope of providing a recipe for translating SysML/UML in terms of intuitive (intermediate) models, for the practical-minded. For a more detailed survey on model checking statecharts we refer to [6].

Structure of paper. In Sect. 2 we provide a brief overview of SysML modelling and NuSMV, by emphasising on the corresponding concepts relevant for our work. In Sect. 3 we introduce the intermediate model used for the transformation of SysML models into NuSMV-compatible inputs. In Sect. 4 we illustrate how the intermediate model can be exploited for the aforementioned transformation into NuSMV. Section 5 introduces SysMV-Ja, a Java-based tool for the automated model transformation. Two case studies, a railway and an airbag system are also discussed. In Sect. 6 we draw the conclusions and provide pointers to future work.

2   Preliminaries

In this section we proceed by first introducing a railway example, used throughout the paper in order to explain our approach.

Example 1 (Running example). The scenario considers a railroad track that is crossed by a street. On the crossing there is a gate, that can close when a train approaches, thus blocking cars from entering the crossing. A car or a train can be in one of four states: approaching, entering, being in the crossing or leaving the crossing. The gate can be in one of the two states: opened or closed. The situation that one does not want in this example is a train and a car in the crossing at the same time, as this would determine a crash.

In what follows, we provide a brief overview of SysML, the modelling language used by practitioners for designing systems such as the one in Example 1. Afterwards, we succinctly introduce the NuSMV model checker–a tool that can automatically detect hazardous situations such as a car-train crash.

The OMG System Modelling Language (SysML). SysML [14,17] is an industry standard for specifying and designing a broad range of systems. SysML was created as a general purpose modelling language for systems that may include anything from hardware and software to staff and facilities.

On the one hand, SysML can be used for the intuitive modelling of systems. We refer to Fig. 1 for a representation of the components of the railway in Example 1, and to Fig. 2 for a modelling of their behaviours. On the other hand, SysML can be employed similarly to a meta-modelling language defining the syntactic composition of the SysML modelling concepts considered by our approach. For instance, **iBDD** and **iStateMachine** in Fig. 3 define the parts (that are relevant for our approach) that constitute SysML Block Definition Diagrams and State Machine Diagrams, respectively.

Intuitively, SysML Block Definition Diagrams (BDD's) and State Machine Diagrams (STM's) are used in order to define the static aspects of systems, and to capture the dynamics of systems, respectively. BDD's are built on top of the so-called SysML *blocks*, and enable the modelling of systems in a modular fashion. Blocks correspond to units of a system description. See, for instance the block **Gate** in Fig. 1, that corresponds to the UML representation of the gate system in Example 1. A block can include properties of certain types and references to other blocks. For instance, the gate being open/closed corresponds to the boolean property "open" in Fig. 1 being set to *true/false*. Moreover, BDD's can capture relationships between blocks such as associations, and dependencies. For an example, we refer to Fig. 3. An aggregation stating that *one* **iModel** (intuitively, the railway system) consists of *one or more* **iBDD**'s (intuitively, the car, train and gate in the railway example) is illustrated via the connector $\diamond^{1}\!\!-\!\!^{1..*}$ with multiplicities *one*: 1 and *one or more*: 1..*.

Fig. 1. The BDD's for the railway in Example 1.

Behaviours can be associated to BDD's via properties of type StateChart. In Fig. 1, for instance, the train is associated a behaviour via the "operation" property. At this point it is important to mention that, in our approach, concurrent behaviour is modelled by synchronising multiple BDD's via *events*. Events occur in the context of *triggers* that specify points in the definition of a behaviour at which some effect can be observed.

STM's, or statecharts, are a form of finite state automata used in order to model the behaviour of systems. *States* in an STM can express different statuses in a behaviour of a system. For instance, the gate being either open or closed is captured by two simple sates "gate_open" and "gate_closed", respectively, in Fig. 2(b).

States can enclose so-called *regions* denoting behaviour fragments that may execute concurrently. Each region contains the nested disjoint states and corresponding transitions. Consequently, there exist the following kinds of *composite* states: *simple composite*–whenever the state contains exactly one region, and *orthogonal*–whenever it contains multiple regions. In this paper we only consider *simple composite* states. A *submachine state* refers to an entire STM nested within the state.

Either simple, composite or submachines, states can specify "entry", "exit" or "doActivity" behaviours. In short, entry (respectively, exit) behaviours are executed when the state is entered (respectively, exited) via an external transition. "doActivity" executes concurrently with any other behaviour associated with the state, as soon as the state entry behaviour has completed. An instance of a "doActivity" is the operation "close_gate" in Fig. 2(c).

Another special kind of states are the so-called *pseudostates*. Pseudostates are states with special behaviour. For instance, the *initial* pseudostate is the state in which an STM is initialised (see, for an example, the three bullet-like initial states in Fig. 2), or *exit* pseudostates. Additionally, the system cannot be in a

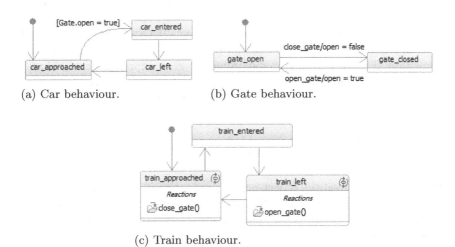

(a) Car behaviour.   (b) Gate behaviour.

(c) Train behaviour.

Fig. 2. The STM's for the railway in Example 1.

pseudostate. As soon as a pseudostate is entered, it is left again in a single atomic step. In this paper we only handle *initial* pseudo states.

Transitions can be seen as valid fragments of behaviour illustrating how the system evolves from one "source" state to a "target" state. A "guard" enables a transition whenever it is evaluated to *true*. We refer, for an example, to the guard "[Gate.open = true]" in Fig. 2(a) that enables the car to enter the crossing whenever the gate is open. The "effect" behaviour is enabled when the transition is executed. The effect "open = false" in Fig. 2(b) sets the value of the gate property "open" in Fig. 1 to *false*. A "trigger" specifies an event whose occurrence determines the execution of a transition. For instance, the event "close_gate" in Fig. 2(b) determines the gate to close. Recall that "close_gate" is also a "doActivity" in the state corresponding to train approaching in Fig. 2(c). Hence, its purpose is to simulate the synchronised communication between the train and the gate.

NuSMV. NuSMV [8] is a symbolic model checker successfully used for the verification of synchronous and asynchronous finite state systems. In short, NuSMV analyses specifications expressed in Computation Tree Logic (CTL) and Linear Temporal Logic (LTL) [5], using BDD-based and SAT-based model checking techniques.

In this section, we focus on the parts of the NuSMV input language relevant for our work. For a thorough description of NuSMV inputs, we refer the interested reader to the user manual in the distribution package[1] of the NUSMV model checker.

Intuitively, a NuSMV *program* consists of a list of *modules* further instantiated to so-called *processes* that model interleaving. A "process" has a special boolean variable associated with it, called "running", whose value is *true* if and only if the corresponding process instance is currently selected for execution. Each module is associated an *identifier* and a series of *parameters*. The *body* of a module consists of *elements* that can denote *variable declarations, variable initialisations/assignments, LTL specifications* or, for instance, behaviours defined based on *transitions*. Transitions are introduced by the "TRANS" keyword, followed by a boolean expression expressing whether or not two states belong to the transition relation. Therefore, the aforementioned boolean expression can include the "next" operator in order to relate the current and the next state variables, and express transitions in the state-machine corresponding to the behaviour of the module.

3   The Intermediate Model

In this section we provide an object-oriented representation of the relevant SysML components we consider for modelling the static and dynamic aspects of concurrent safety-critical systems. This representation serves as an intermediate step in the model transformation from SysML to NuSMV.

---

[1] http://nusmv.fbk.eu.

The advantages of using the object-orientation paradigm include software developers' familiarity with the concept and enables a structured, modular model transformation flexible to further extensions, and appropriate for automation.

The translation of the SysML relevant components into the intermediate model follows naturally. The **iModel** comprises all the elements of the system. All information that is obtained during the transformation from SysML to this intermediate model is either directly, as an attribute, or indirectly, as an attribute of one of its attributes, contained in the **iModel**. Directly contained as attributes in the **iModel** are all components, events, global variables which do not belong to any component, and the properties of the model captured by **iStateConfigurations**.

Each instance of **iStateConfiguration** stands for a safety or reachability property. These properties are expressed by the *configuration states* that shall "never be reached" or "eventually be reached", connected via "AND"/"OR" *configuration operations*.

Another element is the **iAttribute**, representing variables of the system. It can have a *default value*, saved as a string. If the attribute is an integer then it has a *lower* and *upper bound* and a *type* given by strings such as "integer" or "boolean", for instance. An **iAttribute** can be either a *global variable*, in which case it is saved in the **iModel**, or part of a system component, saved as an *attribute* in the corresponding **iBDD**.

An **iBDD** corresponds to a BDD and is characterised by the associated *attributes*. The connection with the STM's defining its *normal* and *failure* behaviours is established via class attributes of type **iStateMachine**.

The **iStateMachine** contains all the important information from an STM: all its *states*, including the *initial* one, and all its *transitions*. A *type* is associated in order to mark the behaviour of the **iStateMachine** as being *normal* or a *failure* one. As expected, an **iState**, corresponds to the concept of SysML *state*. An **iState**, encapsulates the *entry*, *exit* and *during* ("doActivity") behaviours a SysML state can display. **iStates** also include a list of incoming and outgoing *transitions*. If the state has submachines, then they are given by the *submachines* attribute. Note that only the *initial pseudostate* has a translation into the intermediate model as the "intialState" attribute of the **iStateMachine** class. SysML transitions are represented in this model via **iTransition**. The *source* and *target* states are the states from which the transition originates and to which it leads. The *guard* is a boolean formula that enables the transition whenever is evaluated to *true*. Intuitively, *action* collects all changes to attributes that happen when the transition is executed and it encodes the triggers and the behaviour of the transition. Finally, a transition can have a corresponding *event*. If that is the case, then the transition is only enabled if the event was triggered. SysML events are captured by the **iEvent** class which contains the *transitions that are triggered* by the event.

Moreover, note that all the blocks in Fig. 3 have a "name" and an "ID", as they inherit from **iElement**. We omit explicitly depicting the inheritance relationships, for readability reasons.

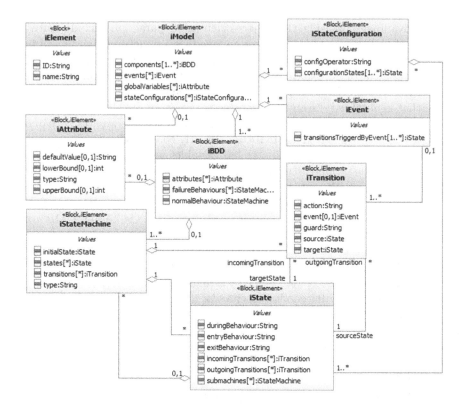

Fig. 3. The SysML intermediate model.

4 Transformations to NuSMV Input

In this section we provide an overview of the translation from SysML constructs into NuSMV input. We emphasise on the usefulness of the intermediate model in Fig. 3, as it enables a top-down, structured approach.

First, the *main* NuSMV module, corresponding to the **iModel** in Fig. 3 is implemented to contain the declaration of a series of modules, as given by its **iBDD** components. Each module in NuSMV is created as a "process". This enables the use of the "running" variable. NuSMV always chooses exactly one "process" for which "running" has the value *true*, and for all others the value *false*. This is useful to guarantee that only one module changes its state at a certain time. Then, all variables (attributes) are declared within the *main* module. The attributes are further initialised with the initial value from the associated element in the intermediate model, or if they do not have one, with the default values. The assignments are performed in the corresponding module of each variable. Relevant fragments of the NuSMV modules and variables declarations corresponding to the railway scenario in Example 1 are as follows:

```
Module main                          Module Gate(g)
[...]                                [...]
  VAR gate: process Gate(self);        ASSIGN init(g.Gate_open) := TRUE
  VAR car: process Car(self);
  VAR train: process Train(self);    Module Car(g) [...]

  VAR Gate_open: boolean;            Module Train(g) [...]
  VAR open_gate_active: boolean;
```

Translations of STM's, or **iStateMachine**s, is less straightforward as states and transitions are strongly interrelated. In the NuSMV code, the state, or the **iState** itself is integrated into the transition system. As illustrated later, state behaviours are translated into variable changes handled in the context of transition executions. Note that we combine the *during* behaviour of a state ("doAction") with its "exit" behaviour, as changes can not be modelled as happening over time.

Moreover, in order to be identified within the NuSMV code, states are numbered in an ascending order. For the case of the gate, for instance, we can declare **VAR Gate_states: 0..10** in the *main* module. Additionally, recall that states in an STM can have a hierarchical structure. In our context, they can be *simple composite*. Assume an STM with three states, out of which one is an STM with four states, as in Fig. 4(a). By recursively apply the numbering procedure we assign, for example, values 1, 2 and 7 to the states of the STM as in Fig. 4(b).

Regarding the modelling of transitions out of submachines: in short, *initial* pseudostates and normal states in a submachine can exit the submachine behaviour at any time. Hence, we translate a transition (with target s) out of a submachine, to one transition (with target s) enabled in each state of the submachine. The original transition out of the submachine is then removed. This transition distribution procedure is represented via the dashed transitions in Fig. 4(b). The soundness of this approach is guaranteed by the fact that each newly added dashed transition inherits the "exit" behaviour and the "doAction" of the enclosing state (numbered 2 in our example). Moreover, each dashed transition has to execute the action corresponding to the transition out of submachine.

Recall that the transition structure in NuSMV is introduced via the "TRANS" keyword, followed by a boolean statement. This statement can be divided into three parts: (a) the transitions which can be executed when the module is running, together with statements regarding changed/unchanged variables, (b) the statement about what happens when the module is not running and (c) a statement to define when the module cannot perform any transitions and therefore has to stop running. In the context of (b), we assert that the variables do not change while the module is not running. Nevertheless, there is one exception to this: if there is a trigger to an event where a variable can change if the event is consumed by another module. Because of the way NuSMV parses a model, all variables that are not changed must be specified as such. This has to be done only for the variables of that module. A sketch-example of a transition system is as follows:

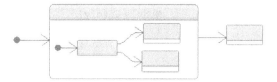

(a) 3-state STM with transition out of submachine.

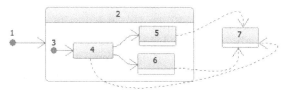

(b) STM with numbered states and distributed transitions.

Fig. 4. Handling *simple composite* STM's.

```
TRANS
  -- (a) When the module is running
  (running &
   (next(g.event) = iTransitionID1 &
   (g.BlockName_states = currentState) &
   (g.BlockName_AttributeName = TRUE) & -- guard for the transition
   -- changed variables
    next(g.BlockName_states) = nextState &
    next(g.BlockName_AttributeName) = FALSE
   -- unchanged variables
    next(g.BlockName_AttributeName2) = g.BlockName_AttributeName2)

  -- (b) When the module is not running
  | !running &
    next(g.BlockName_states) = g.BlockName_states &
    next(g.BlockName_AttributeName) = g.BlockName_AttributeName
    next(g.BlockName_AttributeName2) = g.BlockName_AttributeName2)

  -- (c) When the module has to stop running
  & !(next(g.event) = iTransitionID1 & g.BlockName_states = currentState)
    -> !running)
```

In the listing above g stands for the constructor of the current module BlockName. In the railway example these can be represented, for instance, by self and Gate, respectively. Block_Name_states and Block_AttributeName/Block_AttributeName2 stand for the states and some attributes of the current module. These can be Gate_states and Gate_open, for instance. currentState is the number associated to the current state. iTransitionID1 is the "ID" of a transition. Recall from Sect. 3 that **iTransition** has an "ID" field, as it inherits from **iElement**. As expected, g.event denotes an *event*.

In NuSMV, events are translated as boolean variables. See, for instance, the variable declaration VAR open_gate_active: boolean; in the *main* module. Its value is set to *true* when a state or transition includes a trigger for the event in its behaviour, or to *false* after the execution of a transition that requires the event to be enabled.

An important aspect is that, in order to ensure module synchronisation via triggers, we have to enrich the NuSMV model. In case the module associated with the trigger is not running, the trigger variable has to be handled differently from normal variables because it has to be synchronised with the other modules that consume the trigger. This is done by specifying that the value of the trigger variable stays the same except when the next transition is the event transition:

```
TRANS [...]
  & ( ! (next(g.event) = triggeredEventName)
  -> next(g.triggeredEventName_active) = g. triggeredEventName_active )
```

Regarding the properties of the model captured by **iStateConfigurations** in Fig. 3: note that we are currently handling only *safety*, or *reachability*, specifications. Intuitively, these are of form "never the case to be in all of these states at once" or "never the case to be in at least one of these states". As expected, the former case is modelled via the logical "AND" operator, whereas the latter case is modelled using "OR". Consider, for a generic example, the following:

```
-- if the operator is AND
LTLSPEC G! ((Comp1_states = a) & (Comp2_states = b) & (Comp3_states = c))

-- if the operator is OR
LTLSPEC G! ((Comp1_states = a) | (Comp2_states = b) | (Comp3_states = c))
```

Above, Comp1_states can be, for instance, Train_states, whereas a, b and c denote state numbers.

5   SysMV-Ja at Work

Given a SysML model, the transformation to the corresponding NuSMV input via the intermediate model as described in Sects. 3 and 4, can be performed automatically using the SysMV-Ja tool. SysMV-Ja is a Java application with a simple graphical user interface that enables specifying the path to the XMI file of the SysML model, and the path of the output folder where the NuSMV-compatible input will be generated. The repository[2] containing the tool, instructions on how to use it, and the SysML models for the two case studies discussed in this paper can be accessed with the username "anon".

---

[2] https://svn.uni-konstanz.de/soft/SysMV-Ja/release.

5.1   Case Study: A Railway System

The first case study we consider is the railway system in Example 1, introduced for illustrative purposes. After generating the corresponding NuSMV code, we used the model checker to find a counterexample for the safety property "never car and train in the crossing at the same time". NuSMV successfully identified a counterexample. Even though the generated state space consists of approximately 700 000 states (including those associated to some extra bounded integers from BlockName_states definitions), the reachable states are approximately 300–in the order of what we expected:

```
NuSMV > print_reachable_states
######################################################################
system diameter: 17
reachable states: 314 (2^8.29462) out of 684288 (2^19.3842)
######################################################################
```

5.2   Case Study: An Airbag System

We further consider the transformation of an industrial size model of an airbag system taken from [2]. The architecture of this system was provided by TRW Automotive GmbH, and is schematically shown in Fig. 5. The airbag system can be divided into three major parts: sensors, crash evaluation and actuators. The system consists of two acceleration sensors (*main* and *safety*) for detecting front or rear crashes, one microcontroller to perform the crash evaluation, and an actuator that controls the deployment of the airbag. The deployment of the airbag is also secured by two redundant protection mechanisms. The Field Effect Transistor (FET) controls the power supply for the airbag squibs that ignite the airbag. If the Field Effect Transistor is not armed, which means that the FET-pin is not high, the airbag squib does not have enough electrical power to ignite the airbag. The second protection mechanism is the Firing Application Specific Integrated Circuit (FASIC) which controls the airbag squib. Only if it receives first an "arm" command and then a "fire" command from the microcontroller it will ignite the airbag squib which leads to the pyrotechnical detonation inflating the airbag.

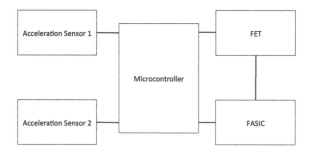

Fig. 5. Architecture of the airbag system.

Although airbags are meant to save lives in crash situations, they may cause fatal accidents if they are inadvertently deployed. This is because the driver may lose control of the car when an inadvertent deployment of the airbag occurs. It is a pivotal safety requirement that an airbag is never deployed if there is no crash situation. Intuitively, the corresponding safety property can be stated as "never no-crash and airbag deployed".

In short, the SysML model (also included in the repository of SysMV-Ja) consists of five BDD's and five STM's, each one associated to one component of the airbag system. The largest STM consists of twelve states, out of which two states with submachines. The remaining STM's enclose at most five states. When running the NuSMV model checker on the input generated via SysMV-Ja from the corresponding SysML modelling, we obtain a state space of size approximately 2^{10}, with about 1 000 reachable states that can be analysed for inadvertent deployment almost instantaneously.

6   Conclusions

In this paper we provide a model transformation from SysML block definition diagrams and state machines to NuSMV input, implemented in the automated tool SysMV-Ja. The procedure takes a file in XMI format, encoding the SysML model, and returns the corresponding NuSMV model provided in an .smv file. The proposed translation relies on an object-oriented intermediate model of SysML, thus making the whole approach more structured and easy to follow, possibly serving as a recipe for other model-transformations. The semantics of SysML exploited in this paper corresponds to the OMG specification [25]. We also discussed the results of model-checking models corresponding to a railway and an airbag system, generated with SysMV-Ja. The reachable state space did not suffer from exponential blowups.

Ideas for future work include the integration of an LTL property editor within SysMV-JA. At the moment, LTL specifications are added by hand at the end of the NuSMV input file. Apart from safety, we would also like to handle liveness properties as well.

We plan to investigate to what extent the translation procedure can be adapted to include other types of SysML diagrams such as activity charts, for instance.

Another interesting extension would be the integration of orthogonal submachines. For the time being, we only consider simple composite ones. Nevertheless, this kind of limitation can be overcome by providing an equivalent modelling of orthogonal submachines via multiple simple composite ones, synchronised via events.

Furthermore, the transformation of pseudostates can be enhanced in some ways. For optimisation purposes, the initial state can be replaced by its descendant, as initial states have at most one outgoing edge and can not have a behaviour. It is a minor enhancement, though, since it only decreases the state space minimally. Nevertheless, such an approach might make the generated NuSMV code smaller and therefore, easier to read and maintain. We would also like to allow "exit" pseudo states. However, we foresee that this would change the handling of transitions out of submachines, as in Fig. 4.

We consider integrating a backward translation allowing to replay counterexamples found by NuSMV in a SysML tool. The formal correctness of the model would be another thing that is interesting to look into. For this, a formal semantics of the intermediate model might have to be created and the transformation rewritten as a set of functions/rules.

Last, but not least, we want to analyse the proposed approach for more case studies, and we want to perform efficiency studies as well. Moreover, we want to perform comparisons with other similar model transformation tools, regarding modularity, adaptability to different model-checkers, and portability.

Acknowledgements. We are grateful to the anonymous reviewers of CyPhy 2016, for their useful comments and observations.

References

1. Hugo/RT. https://www.informatik.uni-augsburg.de/en/chairs/swt/sse/hugort
2. Aljazzar, H., Fischer, M., Grunske, L., Kuntz, M., Leitner-Fischer, F., Leue, S.: Safety analysis of an airbag system using probabilistic FMEA and probabilistic counterexamples. In: QEST 2009, pp. 299–308. IEEE Computer Society (2009)
3. Alur, R., Yannakakis, M.: Model checking of hierarchical state machines. ACM Trans. Program. Lang. Syst. **23**(3), 273–303 (2001)
4. Ando, T., Yatsu, H., Kong, W., Hisazumi, K., Fukuda, A.: Translation rules of SysML state machine diagrams into CSP# toward formal model checking. IJWIS **10**(2), 151–169 (2014)
5. Baier, C., Katoen, J.: Principles of Model Checking. MIT Press, New York (2008)
6. Bhaduri, P., Ramesh, S.: Model checking of statechart models: Survey and research directions. CoRR, cs.SE/0407038 (2004)
7. Breu, R., Hinkel, U., Hofmann, C., Klein, C., Paech, B., Rumpe, B., Thurner, V.: Towards a formalization of the unified modeling language. In: Akşit, M., Matsuoka, S. (eds.) ECOOP 1997. LNCS, vol. 1241, pp. 344–366. Springer, Heidelberg (1997). doi:10.1007/BFb0053386
8. Cimatti, A., Clarke, E.M., Giunchiglia, F., Roveri, M.: NUSMV: a new symbolic model checker. STTT **2**(4), 410–425 (2000)
9. Clarke, E.M., Heinle, W.: Modular Translation of Statecharts to SMV. Technical report (2000)
10. de Andrade, E.C., Maciel, P.R.M., de Almeida Callou, G.R., e Silva Nogueira, B.C.: A methodology for mapping SysML activity diagram to time Petri Net for requirement validation of embedded real-time systems with energy constraints. In: ICDS 2009, pp. 266–271. IEEE Computer Society (2009)
11. Debbabi, M., Hassaïne, F., Jarraya, Y., Soeanu, A., Alawneh, L.: Verification and Validation in Systems Engineering - Assessing UML / SysML Design Models. Springer, Heidelberg (2010)
12. Ermel, C.: Visual modelling and analysis of model transformations based on graph transformation. Bull. EATCS **99**, 135–152 (2009)

13. Espinoza, H., Cancila, D., Selic, B., Gérard, S.: Challenges in combining SysML and MARTE for model-based design of embedded systems. In: Paige, R.F., Hartman, A., Rensink, A. (eds.) ECMDA-FA 2009. LNCS, vol. 5562, pp. 98–113. Springer, Heidelberg (2009). doi:10.1007/978-3-642-02674-4_8

14. Friedenthal, S., Moore, A., Steiner, R.: A Practical Guide to SysML: Systems Modeling Language. Morgan Kaufmann Publishers Inc., San Francisco (2008)

15. Graf, S., Gérard, S., Haugen, Ø., Ober, I., Selic, B.: Modelling and analysis of real time and embedded systems – using UML. In: Kühne, T. (ed.) MODELS 2006. LNCS, vol. 4364, pp. 126–130. Springer, Heidelberg (2007). doi:10.1007/978-3-540-69489-2_16

16. Hansen, H.H., Ketema, J., Luttik, B., Mousavi, M.R., van de Pol, J.: Towards model checking executable UML specifications in mCRL2. ISSE 6(1–2), 83–90 (2010)

17. Hause, M.: The SysML modelling language. In: Fifteenth European Systems Engineering Conference (2006)

18. Holzmann, G.J.: The SPIN Model Checker - Primer and Reference Manual. Addison-Wesley, Reading (2004)

19. Kamel, M., Leue, S.: VIP: a visual editor and compiler for v-PROMELA. In: Graf, S., Schwartzbach, M. (eds.) TACAS 2000. LNCS, vol. 1785, pp. 471–486. Springer, Heidelberg (2000). doi:10.1007/3-540-46419-0_32

20. Kent, S., Gaito, S., Ross, N.: A meta-model semantics for structural constraints in UML. In: Kilov, H., Rumpe, B., Simmonds, I. (eds.) Behavioral Specifications of Businesses and Systems. The Springer International Series in Engineering and Computer Science, vol. 523, pp. 123–139. Springer, New York (1999)

21. Lasalle, J., Bouquet, F., Legeard, B., Peureux, F.: SysML to UML model transformation for test generation purpose. ACM SIGSOFT Softw. Eng. Notes 36(1), 1–8 (2011)

22. Leue, S., Ştefănescu, A., Wei, W.: An AsmL semantics for dynamic structures and run time schedulability in UML-RT. In: Paige, R.F., Meyer, B. (eds.) TOOLS EUROPE 2008. LNBIP, vol. 11, pp. 238–257. Springer, Heidelberg (2008). doi:10.1007/978-3-540-69824-1_14

23. Lilius, J., Paltor, I.: vUML: a tool for verifying UML models. In: ASE 1999, pp. 255–258. IEEE Computer Society (1999)

24. Mikk, E., Lakhnech, Y., Siegel, M., Holzmann, G.J.: Implementing statecharts in PROMELA/SPIN. In: WIFT 1998, pp. 90–101. IEEE Computer Society (1998)

25. OMG: OMG Unified Modeling Language (OMG UML), Superstructure, Version 2.4.1, August 2011

26. Plotkin, G.D.: A structural approach to operational semantics. J. Log. Algebr. Program. 60–61, 17–139 (2004)

27. Beeck, M.: A formal semantics of UML-RT. In: Nierstrasz, O., Whittle, J., Harel, D., Reggio, G. (eds.) MODELS 2006. LNCS, vol. 4199, pp. 768–782. Springer, Heidelberg (2006). doi:10.1007/11880240_53

CyFuzz: A Differential Testing Framework for Cyber-Physical Systems Development Environments

Shafiul Azam Chowdhury$^{(\boxtimes)}$, Taylor T. Johnson, and Christoph Csallner

The University of Texas at Arlington, Arlington, TX, USA
shafiulazam.chowdhury@mavs.uta.edu, {taylor.johnson,csallner}@uta.edu

Abstract. Designing complex systems using graphical models in sophisticated development environments is becoming de-facto engineering practice in the cyber-physical system (CPS) domain. Development environments thrive to eliminate bugs or undefined behaviors in themselves. Formal techniques, while promising, do not yet scale to verifying entire industrial CPS tool chains. A practical alternative, automated random testing, has recently found bugs in CPS tool chain components. In this work we identify problematic components in the Simulink modeling environment, by studying publicly available bug reports. Our main contribution is CyFuzz, the first differential testing framework to find bugs in arbitrary CPS development environments. Our automated model generator does not require a formal specification of the modeling language. We present prototype implementation for testing Simulink, which found interesting issues and reproduced one bug which MathWorks fixed in subsequent product releases. We are working on implementing a full-fledged generator with sophisticated model-creation capabilities.

Keywords: Differential testing · Cyber-physical systems · Model-based design · Simulink

1 Introduction

Widely used cyber-physical system (CPS) development tool chains are complex software systems that typically consist of millions of lines of code [1]. For example, the popular MathWorks Simulink tool chain contains model-based design tools (in which *models* in various expressive modeling languages are used to describe the overall system under control [2]), simulators, compilers, and automated code generators. Like any complex piece of code, CPS tool chains may contain bugs and such bugs may lead to severe CPS defects.

The vast majority of resources in the CPS design and development phases are devoted to ensure that systems meet their specifications [3,4]. In spite of having sophisticated design validation and verification approaches (model checking, automated test case generation, hardware-in-the-loop and software-in-the-loop

© Springer International Publishing AG 2017
C. Berger et al. (Eds.): CyPhy 2016, LNCS 10107, pp. 46–60, 2017.
DOI: 10.1007/978-3-319-51738-4_4

testing etc.), we see frequent safety recalls of products and systems among industries, due to CPS bugs [5–7].

Since many CPSs operate in safety-critical environments and have strict correctness and reliability requirements [8], it would be ideal for CPS development tools to not have bugs or unintended behaviors. However, this is not generally true as demonstrated by recent *random testing* projects finding bugs in a static analysis tool (Frama-C) [9] and in popular C compilers (GCC and LLVM) [10], which are widely used in CPS model-based design.

It would be extremely expensive or possibly even practically infeasible to formally verify entire CPS tool chains. In addition to their sheer size in terms of lines of code, a maybe more significant hurdle is the lack of a complete and up to date formal specification of the CPS tool chain semantics, which may be due to their complexity and rapid release cycles [1, 11].

Instead of formally verifying the absence of bugs in all CPS tool chain execution paths, we revert to showing the presence of bugs on individual paths (aka testing), which can still be a major contributor to software quality [12]. *Differential testing* or *fuzzing*, a form of random testing, mechanically generates random test inputs and presents them to comparable variations of a software [12]. The results are then compared and any variation from the majority (if one exists) likely indicates a bug [13]. This scheme has been effective at finding bugs in compilers and interpreters of traditional programming languages. As an example, various fuzzing schemes have collectively found over 1,000 bugs in widely used compilation tools such as GCC [10, 11, 14].

While compiler testing is promising, when testing CPS tool chains we face additional challenges beyond what is covered by testing compilers of traditional programming languages (such as Csmith creating C programs), since CPS modeling languages differ significantly from traditional programming languages. A key difference is that the complete semantics of widely used commercial modeling languages (e.g., MathWorks Simulink and Stateflow [15]) are not publicly available [1, 16, 17]. Moreover, modeling language semantics often depend on subtle details, such as two-dimensional layout information, internal model component settings, and the particular interpretation algorithm of simulators [1]. Finally, random generation of test cases for CPS development environments has to address a combination of programming paradigms (e.g., both graphical, data-flow language and textual imperative programming language in the same model), which is rare in traditional compiler testing.

Since existing testing and verification techniques are not sufficient for ensuring the reliability of CPS tool chains, we propose CyFuzz: a novel conceptual differential testing framework for testing arbitrary CPS development environments. We use the term *system under test (SUT)* to refer to the CPS tool chain being tested. CyFuzz has a *random model generator* which automatically generates random CPS models the SUT may simulate or compile to embedded native code. CyFuzz's *comparison framework* component then detects dissimilarity (if it exists) in the results obtained by *executing* (or, *simulating*) the generated model, by varying components of the SUT.

We also present an implementation for testing the Simulink environment, which is widely used in CPS industries for model-based design of dynamic and embedded systems [18,19]. Although our current prototype implementation targets Simulink, the described conceptual framework is not tool specific and should thus be applicable to related CPS tool chains, such as NI's LabVIEW [20].

To the best of our knowledge, CyFuzz is the first differential testing framework for fuzzing CPS tool chains. To address the problem of missing formal semantics during model generation, we follow a simple, feedback-driven model generation approach that iteratively fixes generated models according to the SUT's error descriptions. To summarize, this paper makes the following contributions:

- To understand the types of Simulink bugs that affect users, we first analyze a subset of the publicly available Simulink bug reports (Sect. 3).
- We present CyFuzz, a conceptual framework for (1) generating random but valid models for a CPS modeling language, (2) simulating the generated models on alternative CPS tool chain configurations, and (3) comparing the simulation results (Sect. 4). We then describe interesting implementation details and challenges of our prototype implementation for Simulink (Sect. 5).
- We report on our experience of running our prototype tool on various Simulink configurations (Sect. 6), identifying comparison errors and semi-independently reproducing a confirmed bug in Simulink's `Rapid Accelerator` mode.

2   Background: Model-Based CPS Design and Simulink

This section provides necessary background information on model-based development. We define the terms used for explaining a conceptual differential testing framework and subsequently relate them with Simulink.

2.1   CPS Model Elements

The following concepts and terms are applicable to many CPS modeling languages (including Simulink). A *model*, also known as a *block-diagram*, is a mathematical representation of some CPS [18]. Designing a diagram starts with choosing elementary elements called blocks. Each *block* represents a component of the CPS and may have *input* and *output* ports. An input port accepts data on which the block performs some operation. An output port passes data to other input ports using *connections*. An output port can be connected to more than one input port while the opposite is not true in general. A Block may have *parameters*, which are configurable values that influence the block's behavior. Somewhat similar to a programming language's standard libraries, a CPS tool chain typically provides *block libraries*, where each library consists of a set of predefined blocks.

Since hierarchical models are commonly found in industry, CyFuzz supports generating such models as well. This can be achieved by grouping some blocks of a model together and replacing them by a new block which We call a *child*, whereas the original model is called *parent*.

When simulating, the SUT numerically solves the mathematical formulas represented by the model [18]. Simulation is usually time bound and at each *step* of the simulation, a *solver* calculates the blocks' outputs. We use the term *signal* to mean output of a block's port at a particular simulation step.

The very first phase of the simulation process is *compiling* the model. This stage also looks for incorrectly generated models and raises failures for syntactical model errors, such as data type mismatches between connected output and input ports. If an error is found in the compilation phase, the SUT does not attempt simulating the model. After successful simulation, *code generators* can generate native code, which may be deployed in target hardware [1].

2.2   Example CPS Development Environment: Simulink

While our conceptual framework uses the above terms, they also apply directly in the context of Simulink [21]. Besides having a wide selection of built-in blocks, Simulink allows integrating native code (e.g., Matlab or C code) in a model via Simulink's S-function interface, which lets users create custom blocks for use in their models. Simulink's Subsystem and Model referencing features enable hierarchical models.

Simulink has three simulation modes. In Normal mode, Simulink does not generate code for blocks, whereas it generates native code for certain blocks in the Accelerator mode. Unlike in these two modes, the Rapid Accelerator mode further creates for the model a standalone executable. To capture simulation results we use Simulink's Signal Logging functionality as we found implementing it quite feasible. However, for cases where the approach is not applicable (see [21]), we use Simulink's sim api to record simulation data.

3   Study of Existing Bugs: Incorrect Code Generation

To understand the types of bugs Simulink users have found and care about, we performed a study on the publicly available bug reports from the MathWorks website[1]. We identified commonalities in bug reports, which we call *classification factors*. We limited our study to bug reports found via the search query *incorrect code generation*, as earlier studies have identified code generation as vulnerable [1,22].

We investigated bug reports affecting Matlab/Simulink version 2015a as we were using it in our experiments. As of February 17, 2016, there were 50 such bug reports, among which 47 have been fixed in subsequent releases of the products. Table 1 summarizes the findings. Our complete study data are available at: http://bit.ly/simstudy.

Table 1 shows only those classification factors that affect at least 20% of all the bug reports that we have studied. We use insights obtained from the

---

[1] Available: http://www.mathworks.com/support/bugreports/

Table 1. Study of publicly available Simulink bug reports. The right column denotes the percentage of bug reports affected by a the given classification factor. Each bug report may be classified under multiple factors.

Classification factor	Bugs [%]
Reproducing the bug requires a code generator to generate code	60
Reproducing the bug requires specific block parameter values and/or port or function argument values and data-types	56
Reproducing the bug requires comparing simulation-result and generated code's output	54
Reproducing the bug requires connecting the blocks in a particular way	36
Reproducing the bug requires specific model configuration settings	32
Reproducing the bug requires hierarchical models	24
Reproducing the bug requires built-in Matlab functions	20

study in our CyFuzz prototype implementation. For example, many of the bug reports (54%) are related to simulation result and generated code execution output mismatch. Thus, differential testing (e.g., by comparing simulation and code execution) seems like a good fit for finding bugs in CPS tool chains. Further insight that is reflected in our tool is that it is worth exploring the large space of possible block connections (36% of bug reports) e.g., via random block and connection generation. Other insights we want to use in the future are to incorporate random block parameter values and port data-types (56%) and model configurations (32%).

4   Differential Testing of CPS Development Tool Chains

At a high level we can break our objective into two sub goals: creating a *random model generator* and defining a *comparison framework*. We first present a theory applicable to a conceptual CPS framework in this section. Figure 1 provides a schematic overview of CyFuzz's processing *phases*. The first three phases belong

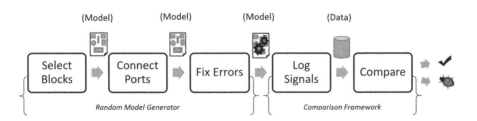

Fig. 1. Overview of the differential testing framework. The first three *phases* correspond to the random model generator, while the rest belongs to the comparison framework.

to the random model generator, and the remaining two constitute the comparison framework. The first two phases create a random model (which may violate Simulink's model construction rules). The third phase fixes many of these errors, such that the model passes the SUT's type checkers and the SUT can simulate it. If it succeeds it passes the model to the fourth phase to simulate the model in various SUT configurations and to record results. The final phase detects any dissimilarities in the collected data, which we call *comparison error* bugs.

4.1   Conceptual Random Model Generator

Following are details on the generator's three phases.

Listing 1.1. Select Blocks phase of the conceptual random model generator.

```
method select_blocks (n, block_libraries):
    /* Choose n blocks from the given block_libraries, place the blocks
       in a new model, configure the blocks, and return the model. */
    m = create_empty_model() // New, empty model
    blocks = choose_blocks(n, block_libraries) // N from block_libraries
    for each block b in blocks:
        place_block_in_model(m, b)
        configure_block(b, n, block_libraries)
    return m
```

Select Blocks. Listing 1.1 summarizes this phase, which selects, places, and configures the model's blocks. The generator has a list of block libraries and for each library a predetermined weight. Using the weights, the *choose_blocks* method selects n random blocks. The value n can be fixed or randomly selected from a range. On a newly created model the generator next places each of these blocks using the *place_block_in_model* method. For creating inputs, CyFuzz selects various kinds of blocks, to, for example, provide random inputs to the model.

The *configure_block* method selects block parameter values and satisfies some block constraints (e.g., by choosing blocks required for placing a certain block). For creating hierarchical models, a child model is considered as a regular block in the parent model and is passed as a parameter to *configure_block*, which calls *select_blocks* to create a new child model. Here n is equal to the parent model, but *block_libraries* may not be the same (e.g., certain blocks are not allowed in some Simulink child models).

Connect Ports. The second phase follows a simple approach to maximize the number of ports connected. CyFuzz arbitrarily chooses an output and an input port from the model's blocks, prioritizing unconnected ports. It then connects them and continues the process until all input ports are connected. Consequently, some output ports may be left unconnected.

Listing 1.2. *fix_errors* tries to fix the model errors that the *simulate* method raises; p is a SUT configuration; t denotes a timeout value.

```
method fix_errors (m, p, attempt_limit, t):
    for i = 1 to attempt_limit:
        < r^p_status, r^p_data, errors > = simulate(m, p, t)
        if r^p_status is error:
            if fix_model(m, errors) is false:
                return < r^p_status, r^p_data, errors >
        else:
            return < r^p_status, r^p_data, errors >
    return simulate(m, p, t)
```

Fix Errors. Because of their simplicity, CyFuzz's first two phases may generate invalid models that cannot be simulated successfully. The third phase tries to fix these errors. Listing 1.2 outlines the approach. It uses method *simulate* to simulate model m up to time $t \in \mathbb{R}^+$ (in milliseconds) using SUT configuration p.

The *simulate* output is a 3-tuple, where r^p_{status} is one of *success*, *error*, or *timed − out*. Note that first step of simulation is compiling the model (see Sect. 2). If m has errors, *simulate* will abort compilation, storing error-related diagnostic information in *errors*. r^p_{data} contains simulation results (time series data of the model's blocks' outputs) if $r^p_{status} = success$.

At this point we assume that the error messages are informative enough to drive the generator. For example, Simulink satisfies this assumption. Using *errors*, *fix_model* tries to fix the errors by changing the model. As it changes the model this phase may introduce new errors. We try to address such secondary errors in subsequent loop iterations in Listing 1.2, up to a configurable number *attempt_limit*. While this approach is clearly an imperfect heuristic, it has worked relatively well in our preliminary experience (as, e.g., is indicated by the low error rate in Table 2).

4.2   Conceptual Comparison Framework

Here we explore simulating a randomly generated model varying SUT-specific configuration options of a CPS tool chain, and thus testing it in two phases.

Log Signals. If simulation was successful in the Fix Errors phase, CyFuzz simulates the model varying configurations of the SUT in this phase; let P be such a set of configurations. Using the *simulate* method introduced in Sect. 4.1, for each $p \in P$ we calculate $<r^p_{status}, r^p_{data}, errors> = simulate(m, p, t)$ for a model m and add r^p_{data} to a set d only if $r^p_{status} = success$. We pass d to next phase of the framework. r^p_{data} should contain time series data of the output ports of the model's blocks at all available simulation steps. In the next phase, however, we use only the values recorded at the last simulation step; we leave comparing signal values at other simulation steps as future task.

Compare. In its last phase, CyFuzz compares the recorded simulation results d obtained in the previous phase using method *compare* (Listing 1.4). It uses method *retrieve*, which returns the signal value of a particular block's particular port at a given time instance. If the value is not available (e.g., blocks that do not have output ports do not participate in signal logging), it returns the special value *Nil*. *compare* also uses method *latest_time* which returns the time of the last simulation step for a given block's particular port. If no data is available, it returns *Nil*.

Listing 1.3. Determining equivalence via tolerance limit ϵ.

```
method equiv (p, q):
 if p and q are Nil: // Missing both data points
    return true
 if p or q is Nil: // Missing one data point
    return false
 return |p - q| < ϵ
```

Listing 1.4. This method compares two execution results (of model m) taken as first two arguments and throws errors if it finds a dissimilarity.

```
method compare (r_data^p, r_data^q, m):
    for each block b of the model m:
        for each output port y of the block b:
            t_p = latest_time(r_data^p, b, y)
            t_q = latest_time(r_data^q, b, y)
            if equiv(t_p, t_q) is false:
                throw ''Time Mismatch'' error
            else if t_p ≠ Nil:
                if equiv(retrieve(r_data^p, b, y, t_p), retrieve(r_data^q, b, y, t_q)) is false:
                    throw ''Data Mismatch'' error
```

Now, taking two elements from d at a time we form all possible pairs (r_{data}^p, r_{data}^q) where $p \neq q$ and apply method *compare* on them. As comparing floating-point numbers using straight equality checking is problematic [1,23], *eqiv* (Listing 1.3) method uses a tolerance limit to determine floating-point equivalence. If *compare* reports an error, we mark m as a *comparison error* for p, q and submit it to manual inspection.

5 CyFuzz Prototype Implementation for Simulink

We have developed a prototype implementation of CyFuzz mostly in Matlab. The tool continuously generates one Simulink model at a time and then passes it to the comparison framework. Source code, implementation and usage details, sample generated models, and detailed experiment results are available at: https://github.com/verivital/slsf_randgen.

Selecting and Configuring Blocks. Simulink itself has over 15 built-in libraries. MathWorks also offers `toolboxes`, which add to Simulink additional libraries. To date we have included in our experiments blocks from only four of these libraries, `Sources`, `Sinks`, `Discrete`, and `Concrete`. We use default parameter values for configuring most blocks. However, some Simulink blocks do not allow placing multiple instances of the same block with the same default value in a model. For these blocks we randomly choose parameter values.

Generating Hierarchical Models. Since hierarchical models are very popular among Simulink users, our prototype can generate them. Currently, the generator uses `Model referencing` and `For each subsystems` blocks to create hierarchical models. CyFuzz generates model hierarchies up to a configurable depth. In doing so it places and configures related blocks. For example, CyFuzz automatically puts input (output) related blocks in a new child model which are used to accept (return) data from (to) the parent model. The number of blocks for the top-level and child models are chosen randomly from user-provided ranges.

Fix Errors Phase. We utilize Matlab's exception handling mechanism to learn what prevented successful compilation of the model. Some information (e.g., the error type) can be directly collected from the exception. Collecting other important information, such as the actual problematic block, can be nontrivial. For example, for algebraic loop errors sometimes CyFuzz has to identify other blocks (e.g., a parent block) to fix the problem. As another example, the current CyFuzz version does not attempt to know the data types of the ports in the Connect Ports phase. Rather, it collects such information when compiling the model using diagnostic information returned by the SUT.

Models with Random Native Code. To facilitate blocks with custom behavior, Simulink allows placing native code (C, Matlab etc.) directly in models. To generate such blocks we leverage Csmith, which generates random C programs [10]. We designed simple Simulink blocks using Matlab's `S-function` interface that use random code generated by a customized version of Csmith. Our customized version is capable of generating many different C functions that can be called from various simulation steps. We looked for both crash errors and "wrong code errors" (similar to our comparison error). However, this is not fully integrated with CyFuzz yet.

The Comparison Framework. CyFuzz starts with varying simulation modes (see Sect. 2.2). And compiler optimization levels. For instance, "`Normal` mode", "`Accelerator` mode; optimization on", and "`Rapid Accelerator`; optimization off" are options to vary. Varying compilers, code generators, solver-specific settings, and other possible SUT configuration options are future work.

6   Experience with CyFuzz

Here we analyze our prototype implementation based on experimental results.

6.1   Research Questions (RQ), Experimental Setup, and Results

Throughout this work we explore the following research questions.

RQ1 Is the random model generator effective? Which portion of the generated models can the SUT compile and simulate within a given time bound?

RQ2 Using the generated models, can the comparison framework effectively find bugs (comparison errors or crashes) in the SUT ?

RQ3 What is the runtime of each of CyFuzz's stages? Does the generator scale with the generated model's number of blocks?

To answer these questions we conducted experiments using Matlab 2015a on Ubuntu 14.10 and varied simulation mode (**Normal** vs. **Accelerator**) and optimizer (on vs. off) for the later mode. For the *fix_errors* method (Listing 1.2) we chose *attempt_limit* 10 and *timeout* 12. For choosing blocks we used a traditional $O(n)$ implementation of the *fitness proportion selection* algorithm [24]. We have not included in these experiments hierarchical models or custom blocks.

Effectively Creating Random Models (RQ 1). As the experimental results in Table 2 suggest, our tool can generate many models that Simulink can successfully simulate. For each row in the table we have a low error and timed-out rate. This high success rate is crucial for the framework as it only uses such valid models in the tool's later comparison framework phases. We also observed that the number of errors and timed-out models varied with the selected block libraries, but we have not yet analyzed the reasons of these variations.

Table 2. Each row represents a separate experiment. Columns 3–6 is the percentage of blocks selected per library (e.g., experiment A chose 80% of the blocks from the **Discrete** library). *Error* denotes the number of models that failed to simulate. *Timed-out* denotes the models that did not complete simulation within the time bound.

Exp. label	Total models	Discrete [%]	Concrete [%]	Source [%]	Sink [%]	Error [%]	Timed-out [%]	Confirmed bugs [%]
A	1172	80	0	10	10	9.73	0.60	0
B	1095	43	37	10	10	1.74	7.03	0
C	1449	0	80	10	10	12.01	8.63	0

Table 3. More information on experiments from Table 2. Columns 3–7 denotes the time taken by the five phases of CyFuzz. *Runtime* denotes the average time CyFuzz spent for a model.

Exp. label	Blocks/ model	Select blocks [%]	Connect ports [%]	Fix errors [%]	Log signals [%]	Compare [%]	Runtime [sec]
A	35.00	7.85	0.64	16.00	74.55	0.96	40.37
B	34.96	6.06	0.39	16.06	76.86	0.63	51.87
C	35.05	8.09	0.51	11.02	79.58	0.80	42.51

Effectiveness of Comparison Framework (RQ 2). We have not found new bugs yet, however, our framework reproduced an existing bug and found interesting cases (see Sect. 6.2).

Runtime Analysis (RQ 3). The Select Blocks algorithm of Listing 1.1 has runtime $O(n)$, n being the number of blocks in the model and using an $O(1)$ block selection algorithm. The random model generator scales linearly with the number of blocks. But as the number of blocks grows, the number of timed-out models and errors also grow. A preliminary analysis suggests that there are relatively few distinct error causes. We group errors by their causes and fixing one cause dramatically increased the overall number of successfully executed models.

Table 3 indicates that the Log Signals phase uses most of the runtime. This result is not surprising, as in this phase the SUT simulates the model, generates and executes code, and logs the data, all of which are time consuming tasks.

Using Native Code/Custom Blocks. In separate experiments we used a fixed Simulink model with a custom block created using `S-Function`. We repeatedly generated random C code using a customized version of Csmith and plugged this code in the `S-function`, which effectively ran the code once we simulated the model. We used different optimizer settings for GCC when compiling and were able to reproduce crash and "wrong code" bugs of GCC 4.4.3. This shows that incorporating Csmith in our framework is promising. However, more work is needed to fully utilize Csmith-generated programs and create sophisticated Simulink blocks using them. One limitation is that floating-point support in Csmith is currently still basic and can only be used for detecting crash-bugs.

6.2   Interesting Comparison Framework Findings

Following are two interesting findings of our experiments, including one independently rediscovered confirmed Simulink bug.

Comparison Error for Models with Algebraic Loops. In our experiments we noticed comparison errors for some models where Simulink solved algebraic loops. Investigating further we noticed that when Simulink solves an algebraic loop it is not confident of its correctness [21]. For this, we did not classify this case as a bug. CyFuzz now eliminates algebraic loops altogether rather than relying on Simulink to solve them. We note that one can use our tool to opportunistically discover such inaccuracies for models with algebraic loops and decide whether to accept Simulink's solution for solving the loops.

Bug in Simulink's `Rapid Accelerator` Mode. In separate experiments with hierarchical models, we noticed that for a model (see Fig. 2) values of a Simulink `Outport` block are significantly different in `Normal` and `Rapid Accelerator` mode. This was detected automatically by our comparison framework. After submitting a bug report MathWorks confirmed that the case was already identified as a bug and they fixed it for later versions.

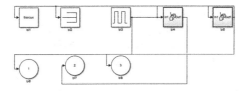

Fig. 2. Screen-shot of generated top-level Simulink model which reproduced a bug

7   Future Work and Discussion

Our ultimate goal is to provide a full-fledged fuzz-testing framework for Simulink. Our work on CyFuzz and our prototype implementation for Simulink are thus both ongoing. Following is a sample of the opportunities for improvement.

The current prototype implementation has several limitations. Currently, the tool chooses blocks from only four built-in libraries. Incorporating additional libraries will increase the expressiveness of generated models and thus its potential for finding bugs. Also, we plan on integrating custom blocks developed using native code and perform experiments we were not able to conduct yet.

The comparison framework implementation is also not free from shortcomings. So far, we have only used various simulation modes and compiler optimization levels. However, we are interested in adding more variations (e.g. those listed in Sect. 5). Finally, CyFuzz should compare signals in multiple simulation steps, since it was also found effective in previous work [25].

8   Related Work

The following focuses on the most closely related work not covered by the introduction section. Existing approaches for CPS testing mostly aim at generating test cases for existing models (e.g., [18,26]) and do not target testing of CPS tool chains. *Code generator testing* [1,27] only target a relatively small component of the CPS tool chain but not an entire CPS tool chain.

Most of the compiler fuzzers perform random walks over a context-free grammar, thus mainly focusing on generating syntactically valid [14] and well typed programs in imperative languages [10,11,28,29]. None of the works target dataflow languages like Simulink. We find Csmith most related to our work, which is state-of-the-art C compiler fuzzer. Csmith leverages the well-published C99 standard and can be used to test only a component of entire CPS tool chain [10]. Our test generation and comparison techniques differ fundamentally from Csmith. Conceptually, CPS tool chain fuzzing is a super-set of the schemes presented in Csmith. CPS tool chains typically contain a C compiler; thus CyFuzz leverages Csmith as a component.

Earlier work includes a differential testing based runtime verification framework, leveraging a random hybrid automata generator [25,30]. Other works attack code generators used in CPS tool chain. Stürmer et al. generate model taking specification of a code generator's optimization rules in graph grammar [1].

But such specifications for code generators might not be available and white-box testing in parts is undesirable [31]. Sampath et al. propose testing *model-processing tools* taking semantic meta-model of Stateflow (a Simulink component) [31]. But the approach does not scale and the complete specifications it needs are not available. In contrast, we propose the first fuzz-testing framework to test arbitrary CPS tool chains based on feasible model generation.

Many CPS model verification and safety checking approaches have been proposed [8,32]. Recent work verifies existing SL/Stateflow (SL/SF) models by generating test inputs for these models [18,19]. Alur et al. analyze generated symbolic traces of a SL/SF model, and combine simulation and symbolic analysis for improving coverage of given SL/SF models [33]. The *Simulink Code Inspector* compares generated code for a given model based on structural equivalence and traceability [21]. However none of these approaches describe random generation of Simulink models for fuzzing the CPS tool chain.

9   Conclusions

This work addresses the CPS tool chain quality problem using a differential testing scheme. Existing work either does not test CPS development tool chains or only tests small subsets. As CPS tool chains are actively developed and released, formal specification based test generation schemes are not suitable for fuzzing CPS tool chains. Rather, our approach follows a simple model generation strategy applicable to arbitrary CPS modeling languages. Starting with a random and possibly erroneous model, our generator fixes various errors in the model using diagnostic information returned by the system under test. In our experiments a high portion of the generated models could thus be executed without errors.

We also define techniques to find bugs in CPS tool chains based on simulation result comparison. The approach is effective as our prototype implementation for Simulink found interesting cases and one bug. Although our model generator is scalable and fully automatic, more work is needed to systematically search the huge space of possible data-flow models and generate those models that are likely to find bugs in modern CPS development environments.

Acknowledgments. This material is based upon work supported by the National Science Foundation under Grants No. 1117369, 1464311, and 1527398, by Air Force Office of Scientific Research (AFOSR) contract numbers FA9550-15-1-0258 and FA9550-16-1-0246, and by Air Force Research Lab (AFRL) contract number FA8750-15-1-0105. Any opinions, findings, and conclusions or recommendations expressed in this publication are those of the authors and do not necessarily reflect the views of AFRL, AFOSR, or NSF.

References

1. Stürmer, I., Conrad, M., Dörr, H., Pepper, P.: Systematic testing of model-based code generators. IEEE Trans. Softw. Eng. (TSE) **33**(9), 622–634 (2007)
2. Lee, E.A., Seshia, S.A.: Introduction to Embedded Systems: A Cyber-Physical Systems Approach, 1st edn (2011). http://LeeSeshia.org
3. Beizer, B.: Software Testing Techniques, 2nd edn. Van Nostrand Reinhold, New York (1990)
4. U.S. National Institute of Standards and Technology (NIST): The economic impacts of inadequate infrastructure for software testing: planning report 02-3 (May 2002)
5. U.S. Consumer Product Safety Commission (CPSC): Recall 11-702: fire alarm control panels recalled by fire-lite alarms due to alert failure, October 2010. http://www.cpsc.gov/en/Recalls/2011/Fire-Alarm-Control-Panels-Recalled-by-Fire-Lite-Alarms-Due-to-Alert-Failure
6. U.S. National Highway Traffic Safety Administration (NHTSA): Defect information report 14V-053, February 2014. http://www-odi.nhtsa.dot.gov/acms/cs/jaxrs/download/doc/UCM450071/RCDNN-14V053-0945.pdf
7. Alemzadeh, H., Iyer, R.K., Kalbarczyk, Z., Raman, J.: Analysis of safety-critical computer failures in medical devices. IEEE Secur. Priv. **11**(4), 14–26 (2013)
8. Johnson, T.T., Bak, S., Drager, S.: Cyber-physical specification mismatch identification with dynamic analysis. In: Proceedings of ACM/IEEE Sixth International Conference on Cyber-Physical Systems (ICCPS), pp. 208–217. ACM, April 2015
9. Cuoq, P., Monate, B., Pacalet, A., Prevosto, V., Regehr, J., Yakobowski, B., Yang, X.: Testing static analyzers with randomly generated programs. In: Goodloe, A.E., Person, S. (eds.) NFM 2012. LNCS, vol. 7226, pp. 120–125. Springer, Heidelberg (2012). doi:10.1007/978-3-642-28891-3_12
10. Yang, X., Chen, Y., Eide, E., Regehr, J.: Finding and understanding bugs in C compilers. In: Proceedings of 32nd ACM SIGPLAN Conference on Programming Language Design and Implementation (PLDI), pp. 283–294. ACM, June 2011
11. Dewey, K., Roesch, J., Hardekopf, B.: Fuzzing the Rust typechecker using CLP (T). In: Proceedings of 30th IEEE/ACM International Conference on Automated Software Engineering (ASE), pp. 482–493. IEEE (2015)
12. McKeeman, W.M.: Differential testing for software. Digit. Tech. J. **10**(1), 100–107 (1998)
13. Lidbury, C., Lascu, A., Chong, N., Donaldson, A.F.: Many-core compiler fuzzing. In: Proceedings of 36th ACM SIGPLAN Conference on Programming Language Design and Implementation (PLDI), pp. 65–76. ACM, June 2015
14. Holler, C., Herzig, K., Zeller, A.: Fuzzing with code fragments. In: Proceedings of 21th USENIX Security Symposium, pp. 445–458. USENIX Association, August 2012
15. The MathWorks Inc.: Products and services (2016). http://www.mathworks.com/products/
16. Hamon, G., Rushby, J.: An operational semantics for Stateflow. Int. J. Softw. Tools Technol. Transf. **9**(5), 447–456 (2007)
17. Bouissou, O., Chapoutot, A.: An operational semantics for Simulink's simulation engine. In: Proceedings of 13th ACM SIGPLAN/SIGBED International Conference on Languages, Compilers, Tools and Theory for Embedded Systems (LCTES), pp. 129–138. ACM, June 2012

18. Matinnejad, R., Nejati, S., Briand, L.C., Bruckmann, T.: SimCoTest: a test suite generation tool for Simulink/Stateflow controllers. In: Proceedings of 38th International Conference on Software Engineering (ICSE), pp. 585–588. ACM, May 2016

19. Sridhar, A., Srinivasulu, D., Mohapatra, D.P.: Model-based test-case generation for Simulink/Stateflow using dependency graph approach. In: Proceedings of 3rd IEEE International Advance Computing Conference (IACC), pp. 1414–1419, February 2013

20. National Instruments: Labview system design software (2016). http://www.ni.com/labview/

21. The MathWorks Inc.: Simulation documentation (2016). http://www.mathworks.com/help/simulink/

22. Rajeev, A.C., Sampath, P., Shashidhar, K.C., Ramesh, S.: CoGenTe: a tool for code generator testing. In: Proceedings of 25th IEEE/ACM International Conference on Automated Software Engineering (ASE), pp. 349–350. ACM, September 2010

23. Goldberg, D.: What every computer scientist should know about floating-point arithmetic. ACM Comput. Surv. **23**(1), 5–48 (1991)

24. Goldberg, D.E.: Genetic Algorithms in Search, Optimization and Machine Learning, 1st edn. Addison-Wesley, Boston (1989)

25. Nguyen, L.V., Schilling, C., Bogomolov, S., Johnson, T.T.: Runtime verification of model-based development environments. In: Proceedings of 15th International Conference on Runtime Verification (RV), September 2015

26. Girard, A., Julius, A.A., Pappas, G.J.: Approximate simulation relations for hybrid systems. Discret. Event Dyn. Syst. **18**(2), 163–179 (2008)

27. Stürmer, I., Conrad, M.: Test suite design for code generation tools. In: Proceedings of 18th IEEE International Conference on Automated Software Engineering (ASE), pp. 286–290, October 2003

28. Csallner, C., Smaragdakis, Y.: JCrasher: an automatic robustness tester for Java. Softw. Pract. Exp. **34**(11), 1025–1050 (2004)

29. Hussain, I., Csallner, C., Grechanik, M., Xie, Q., Park, S., Taneja, K., Hossain, B.M.: RUGRAT: evaluating program analysis and testing tools and compilers with large generated random benchmark applications. Softw. Pract. Exp. **46**(3), 405–431 (2016)

30. Nguyen, L.V., Schilling, C., Bogomolov, S., Johnson, T.T.: HyRG: a random generation tool for affine hybrid automata. In: Proceedings of 18th International Conference on Hybrid Systems: Computation and Control (HSCC), pp. 289–290. ACM, April 2015

31. Sampath, P., Rajeev, A.C., Ramesh, S., Shashidhar, K.C.: Testing model-processing tools for embedded systems. In: Proceedings of 13th IEEE Real-Time and Embedded Technology and Applications Symposium, pp. 203–214. IEEE, April 2007

32. Mohaqeqi, M., Mousavi, M.R.: Sound test-suites for cyber-physical systems. In: 10th International Symposium on Theoretical Aspects of Software Engineering (TASE), pp. 42–48, July 2016

33. Kanade, A., Alur, R., Ivančić, F., Ramesh, S., Sankaranarayanan, S., Shashidhar, K.C.: Generating and analyzing symbolic traces of Simulink/Stateflow models. In: Bouajjani, A., Maler, O. (eds.) CAV 2009. LNCS, vol. 5643, pp. 430–445. Springer, Heidelberg (2009). doi:10.1007/978-3-642-02658-4_33

Ardán: Using 3D Game Engines in Cyber-Physical Simulations (Tool Paper)

Fergus Leahy[(⊠)] and Naranker Dulay

Department of Computing, Imperial College London, London, UK
{f.leahy14,n.dulay}@imperial.ac.uk

Abstract. In this paper we present Ardán, a novel simulation platform using a 3D game engine to stand-in for the real world, providing realistic physics and realistic crowds that can interact in real-time with a cyber-physical simulation. Ardán features 3D device (sensor and actuator) placement, flexible time-control, phenomena-on-demand as well visualisation, virtual devices and native application code. The flexibility, control and scalability of Ardán is demonstrated with a corridor case-study that supports upto 200 nodes running at real-time or faster.

1 Introduction

Despite the growth in interest in the fields of sensor networks, cyber-physical computing and the Internet of Things, developing and testing distributed networks of devices remains a difficult task. Testing and understanding how the environment interacts with a cyber-physical system (CPS) and vice-versa relies upon deploying devices in the target environment and waiting for or creating the desired phenomena to interact with the CPS. Phenomena can include events such as movement of devices or objects in the environment, passive or active interaction with people (pressing buttons, triggering motion sensors), or other sensor events. Thus, performing test deployments can be time-consuming, difficult and expensive to run repeatedly.

To address this issue various tools and techniques have been developed, such as test-beds [5,6,8] and simulators [9,10,12,13,15]. However, existing tools and techniques aren't adequate for reliably and comprehensively testing these devices in the context of their target environment and the phenomena which may occur within it. Current approaches for testing sensor networks and CPS have focused heavily on accurately simulating devices, the network and power consumption, with great success [10,12]. However, support for interacting with the environment is limited, typically performed using recorded or designed sensor trace data. This approach can be inaccurate, unrealistic and is restricted to what was recorded.

In this paper we present a novel approach to this problem, integrating a freely available high-performance 3D video game engine (Unreal Engine 4) with an existing sensor network simulation platform (Cooja), creating an end-to-end simulation solution for realistic testing of sensor networks in their target environments. By integrating a 3D game engine, we are introducing sensor network simulations into virtual reality with a real-time and dynamic virtual world, utilising

C. Berger et al. (Eds.): CyPhy 2016, LNCS 10107, pp. 61–70, 2017.
DOI: 10.1007/978-3-319-51738-4_5

the game engine's realistic physics and realistic crowds to influence and test the deployed sensor network.

Our contributions consist of:

- A novel 3D simulator for testing cyber-physical systems in a virtual world using realistic physics and crowds to simulate interactions with the environment and people.
- An example case study, the corridor, demonstrating some of the capabilities of Ardán and providing a benchmark for future work.

2   Ardán

In this section we give an overview of the main features of Ardán[1] followed by an overview of its design.

2.1   Features

3D design and placement. A key part of many CPS projects is understanding how many and where to place devices within the environment to achieve some desired objective, such as device failure tolerance or sensing accuracy. With Ardán developers are able to easily and quickly augment 3D environments with devices, scale up or down the size and topology of the device network as well as move devices around 3D environments to test different configurations.

Time Control. Unlike in real-world deployments, Ardán developers are able to control time in the simulated world. Developers can: stop-the-clock, freezing both the simulation and world in time, whilst giving them full control over what they see, allowing more time to observe the environment and move between points of interest; slow down time, giving developers more time to observe or control the simulation; or even speed up time, providing desired results in considerably less time.

Phenomena-on-demand. In order to better test and understand sensor network applications in the real-world, developers often need to wait for or even force desired phenomena to occur and then observe how their system reacts. However, exercising control over the real-world can be a difficult and time-consuming challenge, and sometimes not possible (e.g., fire), due to health and safety concerns.

Using Ardán, developers can take direct control of a virtual person or script realistic virtual crowds to carry out tasks, such as walking between points, avoidance, following or interacting with objects. Figures 1 and 2 show people walking up and down a corridor, avoiding each other's path. Unlike using trace data, genuine or created, developers can easily tweak scenarios, such as moving devices, people or adjusting behaviour, to test subtle or significant variations.

Pattern-matching Eventbus. Logging events in a CPS is vital for post-experiment analysis. Our design utilises the Homework Cache [14], an event

---

[1] Ardán, pronounced "awrd-awn", is the Gaelic word for platform.

(a) Over-the-shoulder view   (b) Camera view

Fig. 1. 15 people walking up and down the virtual corridor, triggering motion sensors

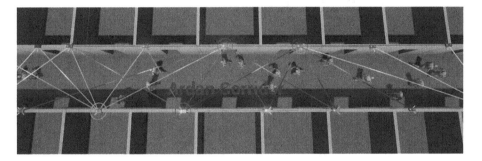

Fig. 2. Birds-eye view

publish-subscribe engine as the core communication mechanism, into which events for both the CPS and virtual world are injected. The Homework Cache provides the ability to perform real-time complex event pattern-matching over the event stream to detect phenomena of interest, such as misbehaving nodes or network partitions.

Visualisation. Ardán provides tools to overlay visualisations of network and device meta-information on top of the virtual world to help understand how the network is running, allowing developers to see information such as how network paths form as packets are sent, as well as transmissions, receptions, interruptions. In Fig. 2, sending devices are highlighted with a circle and receiving devices are connected by an arrow to the sender, each device is represented with its own colour, to help differentiate simultaneous transmissions.

Virtual Sensors and Actuators. Within Ardán we have modeled several basic sensors and actuators, including motion detectors, buttons, lights and location. These act as virtual hardware for the simulated sensors, allowing the simulation to interact with the virtual world. Virtual sensors can be designed to model a real sensor's behaviour, or be virtually improved to provide higher accuracy or more features, not possible (yet) with existing hardware, opening the door to experimental virtual hardware prototyping.

2.2   Design

Ardán itself is not a single component, but a collection of plugins for facilitating the communication and arbitration between different tools, shown in Fig. 3. The individual tools act as peers, sharing information with each other to inform their individual simulations/operations, e.g., location updates sent from the 3D game engine to the simulator, affecting radio transmission.

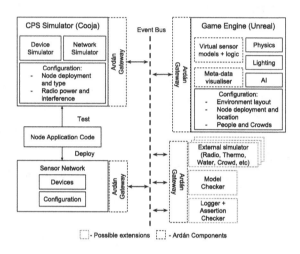

Fig. 3. Ardán architecture

While the goal of work is to build an improved simulation experience for testing sensor network applications by integrating a 3D game engine into the pipeline, we also want to create an architecture that can support future integration of tools to improve the field of sensor network application testing.

Thus, rather than integrate the systems directly, our approach uses an event bus and common schema to describe information passed between the different sub-systems. This approach reduces the tight coupling between components, allowing individual components to be swapped out or new ones added. We envision the use of tools such as model checking, statistical analysis, unit-testing and advanced simulation for radio and environmental properties.

The wireless sensor network (WSN) simulator, Cooja [12], performs all application and network simulation for the co-simulation and is configured with a set of nodes with their 3D location and native application code written in Contiki to run. As the application code is run in real-time, any sensor- or actuator-based hardware requests, such as sensor reads and actuator commands, are forwarded to the 3D game engine to be performed in the virtual environment.

Within the Unreal Engine we modeled a 3D environment and created a several components to support deploying virtual sensor networks, including device and sensor 3D models, hardware abstractions for the virtual sensors and actuators to sense the virtual world and report back to the simulator over the network bus. Similarly within the Cooja simulator we have modified the simulated hardware to communicate to our virtual hardware in the Unreal Engine.

Key features of games engines, aside from the 3D modelling and graphics tools, are their support for advanced physics and lighting simulations. Typically performed by middleware, physics engines, such as PhysX [3] and Havok [1], provide real-time realistic physics including collision detection, rigid- and soft-body physics, forces and motion, fluid and particle simulation, and destruction. Using these tools, game worlds and the objects within react to the player as we would expect, such as objects falling due to gravity or rebounding after a collision. Similarly, games engines also provide advanced lighting, enabling the use of both static and mobile lighting, with dynamic shadows, occlusion, reflection and refraction. Lighting is key to bringing virtual scenes to life, by illuminating spaces, guiding viewers attention and creating natural divisions between areas.

3 The Corridor: A Case Study

To demonstrate what development of a non-trivial CPS application using Ardán, we devised the following case study, based on an office corridor; we show how it helps developers to test and visualise different scenarios using its novel features, and demonstrate its scalability with up to 200 devices.

The case study focuses on controlling the lighting within a modern day office corridor, with the goal of striking a balance between energy efficiency, effective lighting and user comfort. The ideal corridor lighting scheme should provide a pleasant lighting scheme for users of the corridor, able to adjust based on ambient light levels, gradually illuminating as they progress through it, whilst also ensuring energy is minimised by turning off or reducing the brightness of unused or infrequently used parts of the corridor.

Thus, this provides an interesting and non-trivial task, due to the many ways in which the corridor can be entered/exited or moved around within in; people can enter from the beginning, end or from a room; people can move down the length of the corridor or directly from room to room; people often also stop in the corridor, spending time talking or waiting. Similarly, understanding the ideal number and placement for devices and sensors, and how it affects applications, such as power, reliability, robustness etc. Hence, providing effective lighting schemes can prove difficult to analyse and reason without rigorous testing.

The rest of this section will demonstrate and discuss the use of Ardán to design, analyse and test for our target environment, the corridor, highlighting the features and benefits that the tool provides.

3.1 Corridor Setup

We created a virtual corridor within Unreal based on a real corridor within our building, measuring 20×1.5 m, with 5 doors spaced evenly on either side. Along

Fig. 4. Corridor layout with nodes and conical motion detection zones

the corridor we placed 15 nodes with lights and conical motion sensors attached to the ceiling facing the floor directly below, shown in Fig. 4.

To construct the corridor, we used pre-existing models for walls, doorways and lights, making it quick to build the required environment. In addition to these, we created several new 3D models for nodes and a variety of sensors, which can be composed together to create different sensing devices. A drag-and-drop interface is used to place nodes within the newly built 3D environment. The node 3D model is based on a small box with 3 coloured lights, representing the typical LED outputs available on devices, such as the TelosB mote. Each node has a directional light and conical motion sensor attached, giving it the ability to detect when a person moves into range. Nodes also contain parameterised logic to model their functional behaviour within the virtual world, enabling developers to tweak a node's sensing and actuating capabilities to match desired attributes, such as detection accuracy or responsiveness.

The next step was to create the nodes in the Cooja simulator, compiling and loading node application code. Using the IDs Cooja assigns to these nodes, the virtual representations were assigned matching IDs. This is especially important when certain applications are loaded on particular nodes, or when node IDs are used programmatically e.g., for location, routing or ordering.

3.2 Lighting Algorithm

For our case study we developed a basic lighting algorithm which waits for a motion detection event before illuminating its light for 5 s and notifying its closest neighbours. If it receives a message from a neighbour, it checks that it's adjacent, before illuminating its light for 3 s. Using the tool we iteratively developed the algorithm, with the goal of implementing directional path illumination and loitering detection.

3.3 Testing with "What if?" Scenarios

When testing CPS deployments, "what if" questions about how the system will perform will naturally arise, in this case we can ask: "what if we move or increase/decrease the number of nodes?", "what if there are crowds of people?", or "what if we place sensors differently or use more/less sensitive ones?". Being able to quickly test and understand what happens to a system in these different scenarios is key to improving its reliability and efficiency.

In order to test our lighting application we devised several test scenarios based on these questions to test both basic and complex situations for which we expect the system to perform correctly with; the complexity of a scenario increases as the number of agents in the scene increases and the pattern of movement changes from simple start to end directions, thus becoming more difficult to visualise and debug conceptually.

We tested two node configurations, with 5 and 15 nodes placed along the corridor. Using Ardán we experimented with node placement, attempting to find ideal placement strategies to improve the responsiveness and efficiency of the lighting. We found that placing nodes outside of office doors key to ensuring adequate lighting for when people enter and leave the corridor.

(a) Over-the-shoulder view   (b) Corridor view

Fig. 5. Viewing the corridor lighting algorithm from different viewpoints.

We also found by using a greater number of nodes and placing them so that motion detection zones crossed, allowed for the design of a more efficient and pleasant lighting experience. Rather than turning on and off large zones of multiple lights, with fine grained detection we're able to gradually turn on and off light zones, resulting in less lights on at full brightness and a smoother transition from darkness to light. Using Ardán we can also experience this first hand by observing the corridor from the viewpoint of virtual people as they traverse the space, shown in Fig. 5a, or view it from a CCTV perspective, shown in Fig. 5b.

3.4 Crowd Control

When simulating a scenario with a single person, we're able to take control and guide them along the corridor using the mouse cursor. However, simulating multiple people it becomes more challenging, choosing their destinations and ensuring they avoid one another. Using the game engine, we're able to take advantage of its path-finding and collision avoidance tools, to better control and direct crowds of people in a simulation. In this case, within our corridor we placed several target locations which the simulated people systematically attempt to walk to, navigating around obstacles and avoiding one another.

3.5 Performance

To prove useful Ardán needs to be able to scale to support large CPS consisting of tens if not hundreds of devices whilst ensuring synchronised behaviour at real-time or faster. To demonstrate the scalability of Ardán, we used the case study described in Sect. 3, and scaled the number of nodes and running speed of the simulation. Within the corridor we placed the sensor nodes and motion sensors and implemented the algorithm discussed in Sect. 3.2.

The tests were run on the following spec machine: Xeon E5 1650 6 Core with HT, 16 GB RAM, 256 GB SSD and a sufficiently powerful (MSI GeForce GTX 970) graphics card to support the game engine, otherwise, slow response times between the simulator and 3D game engine would cause the simulation to stall and drop below real-time performance.

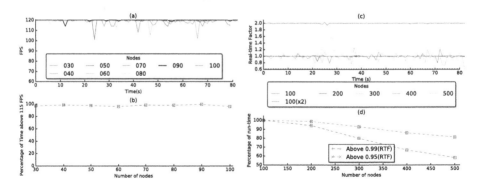

Fig. 6. Plot (a) and (c) show game engine FPS and simulator speed with increasingly large network sizes. Plot (b) shows the percentage of time the game engine stays above 115 FPS. Plot (d) shows the percentage of the total run time which the simulation maintains above 99% and 95% of its target speed.

To understand how well Ardán performs, we measured the performance of the individual components, the Cooja simulator and Unreal Engine, measuring the real-time performance and the frames per second (FPS), for the respective tools. The results in Fig. 6(c) and (d) illustrate the percentage of time Cooja is able to maintain real-time speed; significant drops, below 95%, indicate the simulation is lagging behind real-time, which could cause temporal bugs or artifacts which would not exist in a real deployment. Similarly, for the Unreal Engine, performance is measured in FPS. Regardless of the FPS the engine always maintains real-time peformance; the FPS represents the overall responsiveness of the engine in terms of physics, input, output and networking, thus, a higher FPS provides more responsiveness when communicating with the Cooja simulator.

The results show that Ardán can support up to 200 sensor nodes running at real-time with the simulator staying reliably synchronised with real-time and thus the game engine. Beyond this, the simulator performance degrades quickly and struggles to keep up with real-time. The results in Fig. 6(a) and (b) also show that the game engine maintains a consistent FPS above 115, resulting in a smooth simulation and minimal overhead on the Cooja simulator. We also performed tests on running Ardán at faster than real-time, at 200% speed. In this mode, the game engine and its physics engine match the speed of the simulator, resulting in all activity increasing in speed. The results in Fig. 6 show that roughly half the number of nodes can be simulated in time with the game engine, with minimal fluctuation.

4   Related Work

Previous work on sensor network simulators [2,9,10,12], has focused on creating efficient, accurate and scalable solutions, at a variety of simulation levels. However, they provide little support for controlling or simulating external input into the network, relying on the use of hard-coded input, trace-fed data, scripts or manual interaction with the simulated devices. Whilst useful in some cases, these techniques limit the scope of testing, slow to create/update and inflexible.

Recent work by Mueller et al. [11] demonstrates the use of a 3D game engine for prototyping a closed-loop control system for an electric two wheel vehicle. The work utilises a 3D game engine to provide input/output for simulating the interaction with forces in the virtual world. Similarly, 3D simulation has also been used for design and testing of visual algorithms for robotic traversal and navigation of virtual environments [4,7].

5   Conclusion

We demonstrated a novel approach for testing a cyber-physical, through the use of a 3D game engine to simulate physics and crowds. Through the corridor case study, we have shown how this approach can assist development of applications and is scalable. In future, we envision integrating additional tools to Ardán, such as test and monitoring frameworks, and model checking. Recent innovations in virtual reality (VR) headsets, such as the HTC Vive, also offer exciting possibilities into VR cyber-physical application design, placement and testing.

References

1. Havok. http://havok.com/ (2016)
2. NS1/2/3 - Network Simulator. https://www.nsnam.org/ (2015)

3. Physx. https://developer.nvidia.com/gameworks-physx-overview/ (2016)
4. Agero, C.E., et al.: Inside the virtual robotics challenge: simulating real-time robotic disaster response. IEEE Trans. Autom. Sci. Eng. **12**(2), 494–506 (2015)
5. Baumgartner, T., et al.: Virtualising testbeds to support large-scale reconfigurable experimental facilities. In: Silva, J., Krishnamachari, B., Boavida, F. (eds.) Wireless Sensor Networks. LNCS, vol. 5970, pp. 210–223. Springer, Berlin Heidelberg (2010)
6. Boano, C.A., Zúñiga, M., Brown, J., Roedig, U., Keppitiyagama, C., Römer, K.: Templab: a testbed infrastructure to study the impact of temperature on wireless sensor networks. In: Proceedings of the 13th International Symposium on Information Processing in Sensor Networks, IPSN 2014 pp. 95–106, IEEE Press, Piscataway, NJ, USA (2014)
7. Carpin, S., Lewis, M., Wang, J., Balakirsky, S., Scrapper, C.: Usarsim: a robot simulator for research and education. In: 2007 IEEE International Conference on Robotics and Automation, pp. 1400–1405, April 2007
8. Chatzigiannakis, I., Fischer, S., Koninis, C., Mylonas, G., Pfisterer, D.: Wisebed: an open large-scale wireless sensor network testbed. In: Komninos, N. (ed.) Sensor Applications, Experimentation, and Logistics. Lecture Notes of the Institute for Computer Sciences, Social Informatics and Telecommunications Engineering, vol. 29, pp. 68–87. Springer, heidelberg (2010)
9. Fekete, S., Kroller, A., Fischer, S., Pfisterer, D.: Shawn: the fast, highly customizable sensor network simulator (2007)
10. Levis, P., Lee, N., Welsh, M., Culler, D.: Tossim: accurate and scalable simulation of entire tinyos applications. In: Proceedings of the 1st International Conference on Embedded Networked Sensor Systems, SenSys 2003, pp. 126–137, NY, USA. ACM, New York (2003)
11. Mueller, W., Becker, M., Elfeky, A., DiPasquale, A.: Virtual prototyping of cyberphysical systems. In: 2012 17th Asia and South Pacific Design Automation Conference (ASP-DAC), pp. 219–226, January 2012
12. Österlind, F., Dunkels, A., Eriksson, J., Finne, N., Voigt, T.: Cross-level sensor network simulation with cooja. In: Proceedings 2006 31st IEEE Conference on Local Computer Networks, pp. 641–648, November 2006
13. Pavkovic, B., Radak, J., Mitton, N., Rousseau, F., Stojmenovic, I.: From real neighbors to imaginary destination: emulation of large scale wireless sensor networks. In: Li, X.Y., Papavassiliou, S., Ruehrup, S. (eds.) Ad-hoc, Mobile, and Wireless Networks. LNCS, vol. 7363, pp. 459–471. Springer, Berlin Heidelberg (2012)
14. Sventek, J., Koliousis, A.: Unification of publish/subscribe systems and stream databases: the impact on complex event processing. In: Narasimhan, P., Triantafillou, P. (eds.) Middleware 2012, vol. 7662, pp. 292–311. Springer, New York (2012)
15. Wen, Y., Zhang, W., Wolski, R., Chohan, N.: Simulation-based augmented reality for sensor network development. In: Proceedings of the 5th International Conference on Embedded Networked Sensor Systems, SenSys 2007, pp. 275–288. ACM, New York (2007)

Proving Correctness of Refactorings for Hybrid Simulink Models with Control Flow

Sebastian Schlesinger$^{(\boxtimes)}$, Paula Herber, Thomas Göthel, and Sabine Glesner

Software and Embedded Systems Engineering, Technische Universität Berlin,
Straße des 17. Juni 135, 10623 Berlin, Germany
{Sebastian.Schlesinger,Paula.Herber,Thomas.Goethel,
Sabine.Glesner}@tu-berlin.de

Abstract. Hybrid models are highly relevant for the development of embedded systems because they cover both their continuous and discrete aspects. To master the increasing complexity of embedded systems design, transformation techniques such as automated refactoring play an important role, as they allow for simplifying (sub)models. In safety-critical environments, it is crucial to formally verify the behavioural equivalence of source and transformed target model. For dataflow models that contain control flow entities, this is a major challenge because small deviations of trigger values at control flow elements can yield diverging behaviour of the systems. In this paper, we present our approach that enables the semi-automated verification of the behavioural equivalence of hybrid MATLAB/Simulink models. To this end, we define a static analysis that derives proof obligations to estimate the worst case deviation between model and refactored model. Our approach can be applied to many practical applications such as in the automotive or aerospace industry where MATLAB/Simulink is a de-facto standard.

1 Introduction

Embedded systems are ubiquitous and continuously become more and more important in the near future. Highly advanced manufacturing techniques allow for the production of miniaturised, energy-efficient, highly inter-connected components with huge computing power. This offers the chance to model systems with a large functional range, but also means that the complexity is hard to manage. Especially in safety-critical environments, e.g. in the automotive, aerospace or train industries, it is crucial to fully understand what the system does in every possible scenario. This implies that designers for embedded systems must follow established software engineering techniques. Among these, model-driven engineering (MDE), refactorings and formal verification play an important role because they allow for analysing abstract systems that are safely refined later on. A *correct refactoring* is a model transformation that guarantees that the behaviour of the source model compared to the transformed model is equivalent. MATLAB/Simulink is a tool and the de facto standard for MDE in the above mentioned industries. One of Simulink's important features is the modelling support for *hybrid* models. These are models containing both discrete and

© Springer International Publishing AG 2017
C. Berger et al. (Eds.): CyPhy 2016, LNCS 10107, pp. 71–86, 2017.
DOI: 10.1007/978-3-319-51738-4_6

continuous parts together. Hybrid models allow for the design of the (continuous) environment and the (discrete) control or, in mixed systems, of analogous and digital parts of systems together. Consequently, they are of substantial help for the designer to understand the desired behaviour of the whole system comprehensively, especially in early design phases. However, establishing a formal proof for the behavioural equivalence between hybrid Simulink model and refactored counterpart is a major challenge. The main difficulty is that for the continuous parts, the simulation is only able to calculate approximations rather than performing exact operations. Consequently, equivalent behaviour cannot be guaranteed in the traditional sense in general. We therefore adapted the weaker notion of *approximate bisimulation* for Simulink and provided an approach to verify transformation correctness of discrete *or* continuous Simulink models in [22,23]. This means that we did not yet consider systems with both discrete and continuous modelling elements within the same model.

In this paper, we present a methodology to enable the verification of behavioural equivalence of hybrid Simulink models with control flow. This means in Simulink perspective, the models contain switch blocks with three input ports (two data ports and one control port) and a condition, which is connected with an incoming control signal. If the control input fulfills the condition, the first data signal is fed through, otherwise the second data signal. This case is comparable with the discrete jumps at guards of hybrid automata [17].

As a starting point to achieve our goal, we use the approach presented in [22,23], which enables the verification of refactorings of either solely discrete or solely continuous models using the concept of approximate bisimulation. This approach guarantees under certain conditions (i.e., proof obligations that the designer needs to verify) that the values of source and target model vary within an ε environment. The main challenge we need to deal with emerges if (1) the input signal at a switch is continuous and (2) a refactoring takes place in the subsystem impacting the input signal. In this case, small variations coming from the approximately equivalent behaviour in the control input may result in diverging behaviour at the outport of the switch and consequently at the observation.

Figure 1 shows an example. The control input signal is a sinusoid signal in source and target model that mathematically speaking (i.e., if the simulation step sizes would tend to 0) crosses the x-axis two times. The refactored control signal is the mathematical solution of the ODE in the source model. The data signals are just the constants 0 and 1 to illustrate the principle. The observation at the output of the switch differs as shown in the output graphs below the model. This observation depends on the sample step sizes and the precision ε from the approach [23] as we show in this paper. This means, if certain additional proof obligations can be verified, the diverging behaviour can be avoided, otherwise the designer has to accept a larger ε.

With our approach, we provide an important first step to extend the approach [23] for purely time-discrete or time-continuous models to cope with the problem of verifying refactorings of hybrid Simulink models. In our approach, we deal with hybrid models that patch purely time-discrete and time-continuous

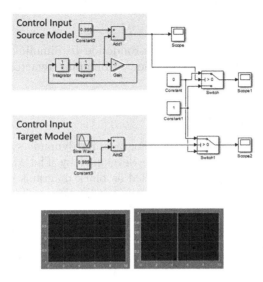

Fig. 1. Simulink example for diverging behaviour: Output

models together via a Switch block. Note that with our approach many industrial applications, are already manageable, since (1) models with time-discrete
control part do not pose a problem (as we also show), (2) models with time-
continuous control part, but no refactoring in this part are supported and (3)
time-continuous and time-discrete data input (refactored or not) are supported.
However, we are confident to even extend our approach to be able to deal with
mixed time-discrete and time-continuous models (e.g. Unit Delay and Integrator
block in one system) in future work.

The rest of this paper is structured as follows. In Sect. 2 we provide some
background information that helps to understand the remainder of the paper.
Particularly, we give a brief introduction to Simulink and to the approach for
proving behavioural equivalence of solely discrete or solely continuous Simulink
models presented in [22,23], which we extend in this paper. Section 3 provides
an overview of our approach in this paper. In Sect. 4, we extend the Abstract
Representation from [23], which is a set of equations that describes how the
blocks modify their incoming signals, and provide a denotation. This denotation
associates the signal lines with the function that expresses how the respective
signal evolves over time - if this is possible (e.g. only if the underlying ODE
is analytically solvable). This also enables us to observe signals from inside a
Simulink model. This is covered in Sect. 5. In Sect. 6, we provide sufficient conditions to check if the behaviour of a source and a target model does not diverge
from each other - or in which time period this can happen - and provide a brief
description of the resulting static analysis. In Sect. 7, we discuss related work.
We conclude with a summary and an outline for future work in Sect. 8.

2   Background

In this section, we provide a short introduction to Simulink and briefly sum-marize our approach for the verification of Simulink refactorings presented in [22,23].

2.1   Simulink

Simulink is a widely used modelling language for dynamic systems. It is based on MATLAB, and both products are developed by The MathWorks [25]. In Simulink, dynamic systems are modelled as block diagrams. They can be sim-ulated, and, with further software packages, it is also possible to automatically generate code.

In this paper, we consider six kinds of Simulink block types: unsampled or direct feed-through blocks (e.g. arithmetic blocks), discrete blocks (e.g. Unit Delay, Discrete Integrator), continuous blocks (e.g. Integrator), sink blocks (e.g. Scope), source blocks (e.g. Constant, Sine Wave, Ramp) and control flow blocks (e.g. switch). Each block can have inports and outports. These are the interfaces via which the blocks are connected.

In [6], Bouissou and Chapoutot defined an operational, synchronous seman-tics for Simulink. It deterministically calculates the values for the next time step for each signal line and each internal variable (for discrete and continuous blocks). There exist two modes for a simulation: fixed step and variable step size simulation. We provide a brief explanation for how the simulation is executed.

Initially, all outputs are calculated: direct feed-through blocks (e.g. arithmetic blocks) are evaluated, the values of internal variables are written on the outgoing signal line. Then, the discrete, internal variables are evaluated. Afterwards, the internal variables for the continuous blocks are evaluated by applying a chosen approximation method, e.g. Euler technique or one of the Runge-Kutta techniques [7]. After this, a *zero crossing detection* takes place to check if the output signal of discrete control elements, e.g. switches, needs to be changed. Finally, the next simulation step size is calculated (only if variable step size simulation is activated) and the simulation process starts again for the next sample step.

2.2   Proving Transformation Correctness for Discrete and Continuous Simulink Models

In [22,23], an approach to semi-automatically show transformation correctness of refactorings for Simulink systems that are solely discrete or continuous was presented. Figure 2 provides an overview over this approach. The idea is that the user extracts equations that describe the effect of all the blocks in a given model. This equation set is called the *Abstract Representation (AR)* of the given Simulink model. The respective interpretation of this AR is an output function (or several if there are multiple output blocks) that satisfies all equations of the AR. This is denoted by $f \models [\![M]\!]$. In [23], it is described that if the user is able to show that the interpretations of both models yield the same values in a given

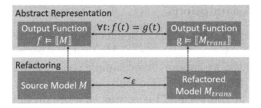

Fig. 2. Approach for correctness of refactorings of discrete or continuous Simulink models

simulation interval $\mathfrak{J}$, i.e., $\forall t \in \mathfrak{J} : f(t) = g(t)$ with $f \models [\![M]\!], g \models [\![M_{trans}]\!]$, then the simulations of both models defined by the operational semantics for Simulink [6] are approximately bisimilar with a certain precision ε, denoted as $M \sim_\varepsilon M_{trans}$. The concept of approximate bisimulation is introduced, e.g. in [11,13]. In principle, it compares states from two labelled transition systems (LTS). The observations of the LTS must be in the same metric space. Two states are approximately bisimilar with precision ε if the distance of their observations is at most ε - and this also holds after one step in both LTS.

3   Proving Correctness of Refactorings for Hybrid Models with Control Flow

To achieve the extension of the approach [23] for solely discrete or continuous models to cover hybrid models with control flow, we proceed in three stages.

1. We extend the Abstract Representation (AR) to cover control flow elements. In this context, we provide a more concise version of the AR, which moves towards a denotational semantics.
2. Our approach is applicable whenever a given refactoring is located in the system that influences the control input of a control flow element (e.g. a switch). If the refactoring takes place at one of the data inputs, the approach [23] is already sufficient. We therefore need a notion that expresses what it exactly means that only the control input is influenced. Furthermore, we define a notion that allows us to observe the inner behaviour of a given Simulink model. In this course, we describe precisely the relations between Simulink models, expressions and interpreting functions.
3. We provide additional conditions and proof obligations that allow the user to verify the correctness of a given refactoring, i.e. approximate bisimulation with precision ε. The sufficient conditions for the approximately equivalent behaviour depend on several parameters that are either determined by parameters of a differential equation such as the Lipschitz constant or can be modified by the user, e.g. the step size.

Limitations and Assumptions

As representatives for discrete and continuous blocks, we currently support Unit Delay and Integrator blocks respectively. All Unit Delays must have the same sample times. Currently, we support fixed sample step sizes only. Feedback loops, i.e., cycles in the Simulink graph, are only permitted with at least one Unit Delay or Integrator in the cycle. This means that we do not support *algebraic loops*, which is a minor restriction because they are practically irrelevant. As control flow elements, we currently only support switch blocks directly. However, the approach is transferable to other control flow elements such as If Action subsystems. Our approach is also only applicable to systems that do not contain time-discrete and time-continuous parts together in one submodel (e.g. Unit Delay and Integrator in the same subsystem).

4   Denotational Abstract Representation of Hybrid Simulink Models with Control Flow

In this section, we extend our Abstract Representation (AR) presented in [23] with a denotation that enables the precise, formal description of the behaviour of hybrid Simulink models with control flow. To this end, we introduce a *denotation* for each signal line, which also defines the behaviour at control flow elements (exemplified using a switch block). To achieve this, we firstly extend some of the notions we already introduced in [23] to obtain a more handy notation.

Definition 1 (Simulink Model Syntax). *A Simulink model is a tuple $M = (B, E, I, O, S, c, s, t)$ with B a finite set of blocks, E a finite set of signal lines, $I, O, S \subseteq B$, respectively are sets of input, output blocks and blocks carrying a state variable (Integrator and Unit Delay), I, O, S pairwise disjoint. $c : B \times \mathbb{N} \to E$ (for connection) provides the signal line at the $n-th$ port of a block (the order of the incoming signal line matters), $s : E \to B$ assigns a source block to a signal line, $t : E \to B$ assigns a target block to a signal line. The subtuple (B, E, s, t) is a graph.*

Next, we enhance the AR and define a denotation for each signal line, which expresses how the signal at this line evolves over time. Note that due to spacing constraints, we move some definitions of the cases in the case distinction to the bottom of the respective definition. Also note that in the following definition, we use terms (set $Term$) in a straightforward way: $in(t)$ to denote functions for incoming signals, $l(t)$ for state variables etc.

Definition 2 (Denotation for Simulink Models). *Let M be a Simulink model. We assign each signal line $l \in E$ an expression $expr_M : E \to Term, l \mapsto$*

$$\begin{cases} in_i(t) \text{ if } s(l) \in I \\ l(t) \text{ if } s(l) \in S \\ f(expr_M(c(s(l), 1)), ..., c(s(l), n))) \\ case(expr_M(c(s(l), 2)) \diamond \xi, expr_M(c(s(l), 1)), expr_M(c(s(l), 3))) \end{cases}$$

Note that in the first case ($l \in I$), also specific functions are allowed, e.g. $\sin(t)$ or even just 1 (constant). The third case applies for function blocks, f stands for the function associated with the respective block $s(l)$. The latter case is applicable if the block $s(l)$ is a switch. The condition in the latter case is extracted as parameter from the Simulink model (the part $\diamond \xi$, $\diamond$ can be $<, \leq, >, \geq$). The denotation of a Simulink model M, $[\![.]\!] : E \to \mathbb{R}^{\mathfrak{I}} \cup \{\bot\}$ ($\mathfrak{I}$ being the simulation interval) is defined as

$$[\![l]\!] = \begin{cases} \varphi \\ in_i \ if \ s(l) \in I \\ case([\![c(s(l), 2)]\!] \diamond \xi, [\![c(s(l), 1)]\!], [\![c(s(l), 3)]\!]) \\ f([\![c(s(l), 1)]\!], \ldots, [\![c(s(l), n)]\!]) \\ \bot \ otherwise \end{cases}$$

The first case is applicable if φ is the unique solution of the ODE $\frac{d}{dt} l(t) = expr_M(c(s(l), 1)), l(t_0) = init$ if $s(l)$ is an Integrator or the solution of the difference equation $l(t + h) = expr_M(c(s(l), 1)), l(t_0) = init$ if $s(l)$ is a Unit Delay. The third case is applicable if $s(l)$ is a switch. The fourth case is applicable for function blocks.

The function $case : Pred \times \mathbb{R}^{\mathfrak{I}} \times \mathbb{R}^{\mathfrak{I}}$ is defined as $(b, f, g) \mapsto f$ if b is fulfilled, g otherwise.

To keep the notation simple, we associate variables l_i with the respective signal lines connected at the output of discrete or continuous blocks in this paper. Definition 2 is sound with the AR from [23]. We omit the proof, which is straightforward, due to space constraints.

Lemma 1 (Soundness with AR). *For a given Simulink model $M = (B, E, I, O, S, c, s, t)$ with finite simulation interval $\mathfrak{I}$, $[\![.]\!] : E \to \mathbb{R}^{\mathfrak{I}}$ is well-defined and if the model does not contain any switch blocks, the following holds: $\forall l \in E \exists b \in O : c(b, 1) = l \Rightarrow [\![l]\!] \models [\![M]\!]$.*

Note that our denotation is not a denotational semantics, since not in every case the ODE or difference equation can analytically be solved, i.e., the unique solution exists and can be represented as expression, and therefore it is possible that some expressions at several signal lines remain unresolved. In this case, $[\![l]\!] = \bot$. In addition, the denotation does not take the approximations into account, i.e., it may map a Simulink model to the exact solution of an ODE. However, as we know from [23], the actual simulation differs from this exact function. As an example, consider the source model depicted in Fig. 1. There, we have at the line l connecting the output (Scope1) $[\![l]\!] = case(\sin(t) + 0.999 > 0, 0, 1)$, since $\sin(t)$ solves the ODE $\frac{d}{dt} l_1(t) = l_2(t), \frac{d}{dt} l_2(t) = -l_1(t), l_1(0) = 0, l_2(0) = 1$. So, in this case we have a fully denotational representation of the Simulink model.

5   Observing the Inner Behaviour of Regular Hybrid Control Flow Simulink Models

Our notion of a denotation for signals in a Simulink model is applicable for both discrete and continuous Simulink models. To achieve a verification methodology for proving the transformation correctness of hybrid Simulink models with control flow, we define a subset of hybrid Simulink models with control flow, namely *Regular Hybrid Control Flow Simulink Models*. This definition enables us to observe the inner behaviour of hybrid Simulink models, which forms the basis for our verification methodology presented in the next section.

Definition 3 (Regular Simulink Models). *We call an expression $f(in_1(t),$ $..., in_n(t), l_1(t), ..., l_m(t))$ continuous if $\forall 1 \leq i \leq m : l_i$ is associated with the signal line at the output of a continuous block in a Simulink model M and $expr_M(l_i)$ is also continuous. Analogously, the expression is called discrete if the same holds for the output of a discrete block and $expr_M(l_i)$ is also discrete. We call an expression mixed if it is neither continuous nor discrete.*

We call a Simulink model M a regular hybrid control flow model if it contains only one discrete control block with outgoing signal l and none of the expressions $expr_M(l_i)$ in $expr_M(l) = case(expr_M(l_2) \diamond \xi, expr_M(l_1), expr_M(l_3))$ is mixed.

Note that with this definition, we ensure that each of the incoming signals is purely discrete or continuous. It is not possible that one of the paths contains both discrete and continuous blocks. Such mixed systems are part of future work. However, a discrete control element, feedback loops, also taking signals after the control element and feeding back in one or multiple of the inputs of the control element are allowed - as long as the requirement that either only discrete or only continuous blocks occur on each path is fulfilled.

In Lemma 1, we linked the interpretation of the AR from [23] with the denotation $[\![l]\!]$ where l is a signal line at an outport (where the observation takes place). This can straightforwardly be extended to allow observation 'inside' a Simulink model.

Lemma 2. *Let M, M_{trans} be two Simulink models, $l \in E \cap E_{trans}$ a signal line appearing in both models, the expressions $expr_M(l)$ and $expr_{M_{trans}}(l)$ both not mixed and without case in it and $\forall t \in \mathfrak{I} : [\![l]\!]_M(t) = [\![l]\!]_{M_{trans}}(t)$. Let furthermore M_l and M_{trans_l} be models that evolve from M and M_{trans} respectively by transferring only edges and blocks from M and M_{trans} that affect l. Then there exists an ε given by the approach [23] such that $M_l \sim_\varepsilon M_{trans_l}$. We briefly write $[\![l]\!]_M \sim_\varepsilon [\![l]\!]_{M_{trans}}$.*

The lemma can be presented more formally by defining more precisely what 'transferring only edges and blocks that affect l' means. However, we omit this here together with a proof due to space constraints.

Lemma 2 can equivalently be interpreted as follows. Consider we take a look at a signal line l and observe the function $\varphi : \mathfrak{I} \to \mathbb{R}$ evolving over time at this signal line (after evaluation by Simulink). If the simulation step sizes go to 0, we would observe $[\![l]\!]_M = f : \mathfrak{I} \to \mathbb{R}$. Consider furthermore another Simulink model with a signal line, simulated behaviour $\psi(t)$ and if simulation step sizes go to 0, we had $[\![l]\!]_{M_{trans}} = g : \mathfrak{I} \to \mathbb{R}$. If $\forall t \in \mathfrak{I} : f(t) = g(t)$, i.e., the observations are mathematically (if simulation step sizes go to 0) equal, then for the simulated observations φ, ψ the relation $||\varphi(t) - \psi(t)|| \leq \varepsilon$ or equivalently $\psi(t) \in [\varphi(t) - \varepsilon, \varphi(t) + \varepsilon]$ holds.

We now have the prerequisites to derive the sufficient conditions for approximately equivalent behaviour in the next section.

6 Proof Obligations for Behavioural Equivalence of Regular Hybrid Simulink Models with Control Flow

We have now prepared all prerequisites to investigate the conditions under which approximately equivalent behaviour can be guaranteed.

As we already mentioned in the introduction in Sect. 1, the behaviour compared between source and target model cannot be guaranteed to remain approximately equivalent with the same precision for the whole simulation interval in every case for Simulink models with control flow. In some cases, time delays in the switch are unavoidable, which increases the precision ε then. To be able to express the time-dependent changes of approximate behaviour as precisely as possible, we write $M \sim_\varepsilon^{[t_1, t_2]} M_{trans}$. That means that $M \sim_\varepsilon M_{trans}$ in the simulation interval $[t_1, t_2] \subseteq \mathfrak{I}$. It is clear that if we have a sequence of n intervals that cover $\mathfrak{I}$ and $\varepsilon_1, \ldots, \varepsilon_n$, then this sums up to $M \sim_{\max(\varepsilon_1, \ldots, \varepsilon_n)} M_{trans}$.

We now present conditions under which approximately equivalent behaviour for regular hybrid Simulink models with control flow can be guaranteed. The first theorem deals with refactorings where the control input is discrete.

Theorem 1. *Let M and M_{trans} regular hybrid control flow Simulink models, the switch block consisting of the control input l_2 and the data inputs l_1, l_3 and the output l in both systems. Let furthermore $[\![l_i]\!]_M \sim_{\varepsilon_i} [\![l]\!]_{M_{trans}}$ for $1 \leq i \leq 3$ due to performed refactorings in both systems. If $\varepsilon_2 = 0$, which means either no refactoring that reduces an Integrator (i.e., resolves an ODE) took place at the control input or the control input expression $expr(l_2)$ is discrete, then $M \sim_{\max(\varepsilon_1, \varepsilon_3)} M_{trans}$.*

Proof. Since the control input is not perturbed, the switching happens in both systems simultaneously and the approximately equivalent behaviour results directly from the application of the approach [23] and Lemma 2.

All subsequent theorems deal with refactorings of continuous control input, i.e., where the control input is perturbed by an $\varepsilon > 0$. The next theorem is about the case where the observation at the input is too far away from the threshold to cause a switch.

Theorem 2. *Let M and M_{trans} be regular hybrid control flow Simulink models, l, l_1, l_2, l_3 as in the above theorem. Let without loss of generality the condition* at the switch be $\geq \xi$. Let furthermore $[\![l_i]\!]_M \sim_{\varepsilon_i} [\![l]\!]_{M_{trans}}$ for $1 \leq i \leq 3$ due to performed refactorings in both systems, $\varepsilon_2 > 0$ (implying that $expr(l_2)$ is continuous), $[\![l_i]\!]_M, [\![l]\!]_{M_{trans}} \neq \perp$ (implying, the solution can be represented by a closed expression). Let the simulations of M and M_{trans} both be performed with the same fixed sample step size h. We also define $\Sigma = \{\lambda h | \lambda \in \mathbb{N}\}$ the set of sample steps. Note that we know that the values of the observations at l_2 for M and M_{trans} vary by at most ε_2 around the mathematical observation $[\![l_2]\!]_M$ (as pointed out in the previous section). We furthermore define a function $Zero : \mathbb{R}^{\mathbb{J}} \to \mathcal{P}(\mathbb{R})$, $Zero(f) = f^{-1}(0) = \{x \in \mathbb{J} | f(x) = 0\}$ the set of zero crossings of the function f.

1. If $\forall t \in [t_1, t_2] \subseteq \mathbb{J} : ||[\![l_2]\!]_M(t) - \xi|| > \varepsilon_2$, then $M \sim_{\varepsilon_1}^{[t_1,t_2]} M_{trans}$.
2. Consider an interval $\mathfrak{L} = [t_1, t_2] \subseteq \mathbb{J}$ where $Zero([\![l_2]\!]_M - \varepsilon - \xi) \cap \mathfrak{L} =: \{\zeta_1, \ldots, \zeta_n\}$ is finite, i.e., the zero crossings are all isolated (meaning around each ζ_i is an environment that contains no other ζ_j) and increasingly ordered. If $\forall 1 \leq i < n : \forall t \in \Sigma : t \notin [\zeta_i, \zeta_{i+1}]$ and $\frac{d}{dt}[\![l_2]\!](\zeta_j) < 0$ with j only the odd indices, then $M \sim_{\varepsilon_1}^{\mathfrak{L}} M_{trans}$.

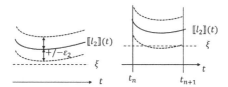

Fig. 3. Illustration for the proof of Theorem 2

Proof. Figure 3 illustrates the proof idea for the lemma. The first case is represented by the picture on the left. The values of the simulations that are within the ε environment around $[\![l_2]\!]$ as described in [23] are too far from ξ to cause a zero crossing in both systems. The second case (depicted on the right hand side) eases this strict condition. In this case, it is possible for the values $[\![l_2]\!](t) - \varepsilon$ to cross the threshold ξ. However, this must not be recognised by the system. Hence, it may only happen between two sample steps. The condition $\frac{d}{dt}[\![l_2]\!](\zeta_j) < 0$ ensures that the crossing takes place starting with an observation from above ξ (note that $[\![l_2]\!]$ is indeed differentiable).

We now describe the cases where the control input signal crosses the threshold ξ completely. If this happens fast enough, we don't have a phase of increased ε, otherwise we have a time delay in the switching and therefore must accept a temporary increase of the error in the resulting behaviour.

Theorem 3. *Let M and M_{trans} be regular hybrid control flow Simulink models, $l, l_1, l_2, l_3, \xi, \varepsilon_i, \Sigma, Zero$ as in the above theorems, $\varepsilon_2 > 0$. Let without loss of* *generality the condition at the switch $\geq \xi$. Consider we have an isolated element* $\zeta^- \in Zero(\llbracket l_2 \rrbracket_M - \varepsilon_2 - \xi) =: Zero^-$. *Consider furthermore there exists an element* $\zeta^+ \in Zero(\llbracket l_2 \rrbracket_M + \varepsilon_2 - \xi) =: Zero^+$ *that follows directly after* ζ^- *(and no other element from* $Zero^-$ *between). Consider furthermore that we have a* t_0, t_n *such that* $M \sim_{\varepsilon_1}^{[t_0, t_n]} M_{trans}$ *and* $t_n \in \Sigma$ *is directly before* ζ^- *(meaning no other* $t \in \Sigma$ *between).*

1. *If* $\forall 1 \leq i \leq n : \forall t \in \Sigma : t \notin [\zeta_i^-, \zeta_i^+]$ *and* $\frac{d}{dt}\llbracket l_2 \rrbracket(\zeta_i^-) < 0$ *then* $M \sim_{\varepsilon_1}^{[t_0, t_n]}$ M_{trans} *and* $M \sim_{\varepsilon_3}^{[t_{n+1}, t_{n+m}]} M_{trans}$ *for an* $m > 1$. *This means, the switch happens immediately in both models. Just the precisions of the relevant input lines must be updated.*
2. *If there are* $t \in \Sigma \cap [\zeta_i^-, \zeta_i^+]$ *(let us say* $t_{n+1}, \ldots, t_{n+\nu}$*) and* $\exists \tau$ *as in the previous item, then* $M \sim_{\varepsilon_1}^{[t_0, t_n]} M_{trans}$, $M \sim_{\varepsilon_3}^{[t_{n+\nu+1}, t_{n+m}]} M_{trans}$ *for an* $m > \nu$. *However, in the interval* $[t_{n+1}, t_{n+\nu}] =: \mathfrak{L}$, *we only have* $M \sim_{\varepsilon_\mathfrak{L}}^{\mathfrak{L}} M_{trans}$ *with* $\varepsilon_\mathfrak{L} := ||\llbracket l_1 \rrbracket_M - \llbracket l_3 \rrbracket_M|| + \varepsilon_1 + \varepsilon_3$. *This means, the switching may be time-delayed.*

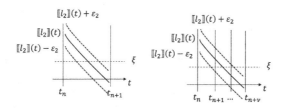

Fig. 4. Illustration for the proof of Theorem 3

Proof. Figure 4 illustrates the proof.

The left image shows the first case in the theorem. The idea is that due to the fact that the values for the simulations at the control input l_2 may vary in the area of $\pm \varepsilon_2$ around $\llbracket l_2 \rrbracket$, the crossing of the threshold ξ must take place for both curves $\llbracket l_2 \rrbracket - \varepsilon_2$ and $\llbracket l_2 \rrbracket + \varepsilon_2$ before another sample step is reached. If this cannot be guaranteed (right hand side picture), the switch may happen time-delayed and therefore an approximation $\varepsilon_\mathfrak{L}$, which consists of the sum of all differences, can only be guaranteed.

The complexity of the proof obligation can be reduced to make it easier for verification.

Corollary 1. *The first condition of Theorem 3 is fulfilled if* $\llbracket l_2 \rrbracket(t_n) - \varepsilon_2 - \xi > 0 \wedge \forall t \in [t_n, t_{n+1}] : \frac{d}{dt}\llbracket l_2 \rrbracket(t) < -\frac{2\varepsilon_2}{h}$. *The second condition is fulfilled if the same term is* $< -\frac{2\varepsilon_2}{\nu h}$.

Proof. For the first condition it is sufficient to check if at sample step t_n just before the crossing, we are still above the threshold and if the distance to the threshold, namely $\llbracket l_2 \rrbracket(t_n) - \varepsilon_2 - \xi > \llbracket l_2 \rrbracket(t_{n+1}) + \varepsilon_2 - \xi$, since the second term (after $>$ needs to be below the threshold 0). This inequality can be transformed to $-\frac{2\varepsilon_2}{h} > \frac{[\![l_2]\!](t_{n+1})-[\![l_2]\!](t_n)}{h}$, which is fulfilled if the derivative $\frac{d}{dt}[\![l_2]\!](t) < \frac{-2\varepsilon_2}{h}$ in the whole interval between t_n and t_{n+1}. The second condition follows analogously.

This corollary is especially helpful if M_{trans} expresses the analytic solution of M because in this case, we can calculate $\frac{d}{dt}[\![l_2]\!]$ easily.

Finally, we provide a criterion if we have non-isolated zero crossings.

Theorem 4. *Let M and M_{trans} be regular hybrid control flow Simulink models, $l, l_1, l_2, l_3, \xi, \varepsilon_i, \Sigma, Zero$ as in the above theorems, $\varepsilon_2 > 0$. Let without loss of generality the condition at the switch $\geq \xi$. If $Zero([\![l_2]\!] - \varepsilon_2 - \xi)$ consists of an interval $[t_1, t_2]$ (i.e., non-isolated zero crossings) and $\forall t \in \Sigma : t \notin [t_1, t_2]$, then $M \sim_{\varepsilon_1} M_{trans}^{\mathfrak{L}}$ for an interval $[t_1, t_2] \subseteq \mathfrak{L} \subseteq \mathfrak{I}$.*

Proof. The proof is analogous to the proof of Theorem 2. If the zero crossing does not coincide with a sample step, it is just not being recognised and therefore the switch does not happen and the precision remains.

Note that if the interval of non-isolated zero-crossings contains sample steps, we cannot guarantee that the precisions of approximately equivalent behaviour remains at ε_1 or ε_3 in general. In this case, only the precision that sums up all distances could be guaranteed.

The statements in the theorems can be used to perform a static analysis to obtain the global precision ε for the approximately equivalent behaviour of the hybrid systems straightforwardly. The conditions can be verified with the help of a Computer Algebra System (CAS), e.g. the Reduce and Resolve commands in Mathematica. Note that since the precision measures ε are actually functions of the form $\varepsilon(t, L, h)$, the user has the option to decrease the simulation step size in order to obtain a better result and consequently yield approximately equivalent behaviour of a desired precision or at least reduce the interval for the time-delayed diverging behaviour to an acceptable period.

As an example, consider the simple Simulink model from Fig. 1 without the part $+0.999$ for simplicity, the threshold at the switch being 0. The ODE associated with the control input is $\frac{d}{dt}l_2(t) = l_1(t), \frac{d}{dt}l_1(t) = -l_2(t), l_1(0) = 1, l_2(0) = 0$. The solution is $l_2(t) = \sin(t)$. This is expressed in the transformed model. The perturbation ε_2 depends on the selected approximation method chosen in Simulink. The set $Zero := Zero([\![l_2]\!]) = Zero(\sin(t)) = \{k\pi | k \in \mathbb{Z}\}$. The set $Zero(\sin(t) - \varepsilon_2)$ shifts these zero crossings a bit to the left (depending on the actual value of ε_2, which depends on the chosen approximation method). The user must then verify that the sample step sizes $nh \notin Zero$ or potentially weaken this and find out how many sample step sizes are in $Zero \cap \Sigma$ to apply one of the cases of Theorem 3 with the help of a Computer Algebra System.

7   Related Work

For the design and application of refactorings in Simulink, several approaches exist. In [18], a taxonomy of model mutations is defined. In [3], a normalisation of

Simulink models is presented, which is used for clone detection in [9]. In [27], the authors present Simulink refactorings that allow subsystem and signal shifting in arbitrary layers. None of these approaches consider behavioural equivalence or correctness of the transformation.

There exists a broad variety of verification approaches for hybrid models, for a detailed introduction see for example [11–13,19,28]. In these papers, the notion of approximate bisimulation is introduced and utilised. Furthermore, in [4] abstractions of hybrid systems are introduced. There, hybrid systems are abstracted to purely discrete systems. [26] provides an overview over abstractions on hybrid systems. However, these works consider hybrid systems in general, with no reference to the semantics of Simulink and its characteristics. Another interesting approach for conformance in hybrid models is [1]. There, the authors introduce a new notion of approximately equivalent behaviour, which takes time step distances besides the distances of values into account. Furthermore, the authors calculate the conformance, i.e., approximately equivalent behaviour, based on running tests, e.g. between simulated model and generated code. However, they do not aim at refactorings at model level and do not consider behavioural equivalence on symbolic expressions on model level.

To reason about correctness for Simulink refactorings, a clear understanding of the Simulink semantics is required. However, the Mathworks documentation [25] defines the Simulink semantics only informally. Existing approaches for the formal verification of Simulink models typically overcome this problem by using transformations into some well-established formal language. For example, in [15], Simulink models are mapped to UCLID and the SMT (satisfiability modulo theories) solver UCLID is used for verification. In [8], this is done with the synchronous data flow language LUSTRE. In [5], an approach for contract based verification is presented. In this approach, the semantics is described via synchronous data flow graphs. In [21], the authors use Boogie, a verification framework developed at Microsoft Research, for verification. In [2], Simulink models are translated to hybrid automata. This enables further investigation of hybrid automata semantics, e.g., in [10] or [17]. However, none of these approaches provides a comprehensive semantics of Simulink. To the best of our knowledge, only [6] provides a direct and comprehensive formalisation of the Simulink semantics. In [22,23], a first methodology to show correctness of refactorings of Simulink models that are solely discrete or continuous was provided. It is based on the formal operational semantics from [6]. There, a set of syntactical equations as an abstract representation from the Simulink models is derived, which describes the changes of signals over time on an abstract level. To deal with the challenge that traditional equivalence notions such as bisimulation are not suitable, the authors adapted the concept of approximate bisimulation.

Since there are no methodologies showing the correctness of Simulink refactorings, also to the best of our knowledge no approach dealing with Simulink models with control flow exists. There are some theories that are related with this topic, e.g. [14,16,20]. They all deal with stability and robustness, i.e., under which conditions hybrid systems do not show diverging behaviour under perturbation. The basis of these works is the Lyapunov stability theory [24]. However, they neither aim at Simulink nor deal with the behavioural equivalence of the models.

8   Conclusion and Future Work

In this paper, we have presented a methodology for proving the correctness of refactorings for hybrid Simulink models with control flow. We have achieved this by extending the approach from [22, 23]. In particular, we have sharpened the notion of the abstract representation and have defined a denotation, which expresses the result of the simulation as a function at each signal. This denotation also allows us to observe inner behaviour in the Simulink model. We also have defined which kind of models we support. Finally, we have provided sufficient conditions for approximate equivalent behaviour for regular Simulink models with control flow. Our approach is able to cover a large variety of industrially relevant models.

In future work, we aim at automating the approach. We were already successful in verifying correctness of transformations for purely discrete and continuous systems with the approach [23]. We plan to extend this to cover the approach in this paper as well. Furthermore, we plan to extend the presented approach by taking variable step size simulations into account. Our approach is already applicable for a broad variety of systems. However, for the continuous parts, it relies mainly on systems where the ODEs may be solved. We plan to strengthen our approach by providing assistance for systems with continuous parts that are not necessarily analytically solvable.

References

1. Abbas, H., Hoxha, B., Fainekos, G., Deshmukh, J.V., Kapinski, J., Ueda, K.: Conformance testing as falsification for cyber-physical systems (2014). arXiv preprint arXiv:1401.5200
2. Agrawal, A., Simon, G., Karsai, G.: Semantic translation of simulink/stateflow models to hybrid automata using graph transformations. Electron. Notes Theoret. Comput. Sci. **109**, 43–56 (2004)
3. Al-Batran, B., Schätz, B., Hummel, B.: Semantic clone detection for model-based development of embedded systems. In: Whittle, J., Clark, T., Kühne, T. (eds.) MODELS 2011. LNCS, vol. 6981, pp. 258–272. Springer, Heidelberg (2011). doi:10.1007/978-3-642-24485-8_19
4. Alur, R., Henzinger, T.A., Lafferriere, G., Pappas, G.J.: Discrete abstractions of hybrid systems. Proc. IEEE **88**(7), 971–984 (2000)
5. Boström, P.: Contract-based verification of Simulink models. In: Qin, S., Qiu, Z. (eds.) ICFEM 2011. LNCS, vol. 6991, pp. 291–306. Springer, Heidelberg (2011). doi:10.1007/978-3-642-24559-6_21
6. Bouissou, O., Chapoutot, A.: An operational semantics for Simulink's simulation engine. In: ACM SIGPLAN Notices, vol. 47, no. 5, pp. 129–138 (2012)

7. Butcher, J.C.: Numerical Methods for Ordinary Differential Equations, 2nd edn. Wiley, Chichester (2008). http://site.ebrary.com/lib/alltitles/docDetail.action?docID=10232593
8. Caspi, P.: Translating discrete-time Simulink to Lustre. ACM Trans. Embed. Comput. Syst. (TECS) **4**, 779–818 (2005). New York
9. Deissenboeck, F., Hummel, B., Juergens, E., Pfaehler, M., Schaetz, B.: Model clone detection in practice. In: Proceedings of 4th International Workshop on Software Clones, pp. 57–64. ACM, New York (2010)
10. Edalat, A., Pattinson, D.: Denotational semantics of hybrid automata. In: Aceto, L., Ingólfsdóttir, A. (eds.) FoSSaCS 2006. LNCS, vol. 3921, pp. 231–245. Springer, Heidelberg (2006). doi:10.1007/11690634_16
11. Girard, A.: Approximate bisimulations for constrained linear systems. Automatica **43**, 1307–1317 (2005)
12. Girard, A., Pappas, G.J.: Approximate bisimulations for nonlinear dynamical systems. In: Decision and Control, 2005 and 2005 European Control Conference, CDC-ECC 2005, pp. 684–689. IEEE (2005)
13. Girard, A., Pappas, G.J.: Approximate bisimulation: a bridge between computer science and control theory. Eur. J. Control **17**(5), 568–578 (2011)
14. Goebel, R., Sanfelice, R.G., Teel, A.R.: Hybrid Dynamical Systems: Modeling, Stability, and Robustness. Princeton University Press, Princeton (2012)
15. Herber, P., Reicherdt, R., Bittner, P.: Bit-precise formal verification of discrete-time MATLAB/Simulink models using SMT solving. In: Proceedings of EMSOFT 2013, Proceedings of 11th ACM International Conference on Embedded Software. IEEE Press (2013)
16. Lazar, M.: Model predictive control of hybrid systems: stability and robustness. Dissertation, Technische Universiteit Eindhoven, Eindhoven (2006)
17. Lee, E.A., Zheng, H.: Operational semantics of hybrid systems. In: Morari, M., Thiele, L. (eds.) HSCC 2005. LNCS, vol. 3414, pp. 25–53. Springer, Heidelberg (2005). doi:10.1007/978-3-540-31954-2_2
18. Matthew, S.: Towards a taxonomy for Simulink model mutations. In: 2014 IEEE 7th International Conference on Software Testing, Verification and Validation Workshops (ICSTW), pp. 206–215. IEEE (2014)
19. Pappas, G.J.: Bisimilar linear systems. Automatica **39**(12), 2035–2047 (2003)
20. Pettersson, S., Lennartson, B.: Stability and robustness for hybrid systems. In: Proceedings of 35th IEEE Conference on Decision and Control. IEEE (1996)
21. Reicherdt, R., Glesner, S.: Formal verification of discrete-time MATLAB/Simulink models using Boogie. In: Giannakopoulou, D., Salaün, G. (eds.) SEFM 2014. LNCS, vol. 8702, pp. 190–204. Springer, Heidelberg (2014). doi:10.1007/978-3-319-10431-7_14
22. Schlesinger, S., Herber, P., Göthel, T., Glesner, S.: Towards the verification of refactorings of hybrid Simulink models. In: Lisitsa, A., Nemytyk, A., Pettorossi, A. (eds.) Proceedings of 3rd International Workshop on Verification and Program Transformation, EPTCS, vol. 199, p. 69 (2015). http://eptcs.web.cse.unsw.edu.au/content.cgi?VPT2015#EPTCS199.5
23. Schlesinger, S., Herber, P., Göthel, T., Glesner, S.: Proving Transformation Correctness of Refactorings for Discrete and Continuous Simulink Models (2016)
24. Teschl, G.: Ordinary Differential Equations and Dynamical Systems, Graduate Studies in Mathematics, vol. 140. American Mathematical Society, Providence (2012)
25. The MathWorks Inc.: Simulink documentation website. http://de.mathworks.com/help/simulink/

26. Tiwari, A.: Abstractions for hybrid systems. Form. Methods Syst. Des. **32**(1), 57–83 (2008)
27. Tran, Q.M., Wilmes, B., Dziobek, C.: Refactoring of Simulink diagrams via composition of transformation steps. In: ICSEA 2013, 8th International Conference on Software Engineering Advances, pp. 140–145 (2013)
28. Van der Schaft, A.J.: Equivalence of dynamical systems by bisimulation. IEEE Trans. Autom. Control **49**(12), 2160–2172 (2004)

Automated Verification of Switched Systems Using Hybrid Identification

Stefan Schwab[1(✉)], Bernd Holzmüller[2], and Sören Hohmann[1]

[1] Institute of Control Systems, Karlsruhe Institute of Technology,
76131 Karlsruhe, Germany
stefan.schwab@kit.edu
[2] ITK-Engineering, 70565 Stuttgart, Germany

Abstract. Verification of switched systems has to include the continuous trajectories as well as the discrete states of the system. For strongly interconnected systems with mutual dependencies it is not sufficient to verify the two system parts individually. It is necessary to examine the combined behaviour in such a setting. The approach presented in this paper is based on the well known concept of using system identification methods for verification which is extended to switched systems. The authors introduce the idea to tackle the verification of complex mechatronical systems as hybrid identification problem. Therefore the specification is given by the user in terms of the parameters of linear dynamic systems and a superimposed state machine. The implemented system under test can be transformed into the same representation using input/output measurement data and a recently developed hybrid identification procedure. Finally it is possible to compare the two representations automatically and calculate a formal statement about the consistency between specification and implementation.

Keywords: Test automation · Hybrid identification · Switched systems

1 Introduction

Testing is still a time and resources consuming activity based on the expert knowledge of the responsible engineer [22,32]. While this was a feasible solution in the past, the growing complexity of current and future systems renders the manual approach impossible. Especially the combination of discrete and continuous system parts to systems showing hybrid behaviour leads to verification questions that are not solved today [28,32]. Even though there is no satisfying solution available, the problem is present in the everyday engineering practice.

The unsolved verification[1] question is given as follows: Is the behaviour of a given System under Test (SUT) - composed of a time continuous plant and its controller - consistent with the given specification? Does this consistency hold

---

[1] The term "verification" is used in the control engineering sense throughout this paper which is denoted as "conformance testing" in computer science.

© Springer International Publishing AG 2017
C. Berger et al. (Eds.): CyPhy 2016, LNCS 10107, pp. 87–100, 2017.
DOI: 10.1007/978-3-319-51738-4_7

for all possible excitation signals and during all discrete states of the resulting hybrid system?

One possible solution is to tackle the controller and the plant individually. Focusing on the discrete verification problem of the embedded controller, there are several automatic verification methods available [10,30]. Those methods are concerned with properties of the controller code (e.g. semantic correctness or determination of loops) [7,12,13] or runtime errors (e.g. overflow, divide by zero, out of bounds array access and others) [18,27]. Some of these properties can be determined automatically using theorem prover or model checker [32].

As the behaviour of the overall system is given by the controller and the plant, focusing on the discrete part is not enough. There are systematic approaches for the verification of hybrid systems based on the so called "state space exploration" principle or "reachability analysis" [3,4,9,12,13]. A sound review of current state of the art reachability analysis tools is given in [28]. The basic idea is to discretize the regarded space and run simulations using different combinations of the values until a given coverage criterion is fulfilled [12]. To constrain the number of necessary simulations, equivalence classes can be formed [2,8,12,31]. Equivalence classes combine input values that lead to the same result. Thereby is the correct behaviour of one representative used to reason about the correct behaviour of the whole equivalence class. Another possibility is to use additional knowledge about the system or the user of the system to extract excitation signals that are very likely to occur during operation (statistical testing, scenario testing) [13,19].

When regarding continuous subsystems the discretization has to be very fine over the whole signal range thus prohibiting the use of equivalence classes and increasing the necessary computation time [6,12]. This is due to the fact that it is not sufficient to check one specific, time constant value of an equivalence class any more. The whole continuous dynamic trajectory has to be taken into account to allow a profound verification [6]. Signal based features like maximum values or static tolerances can be verified using temporal logics as shown in [22].

Other hybrid verification approaches use Simulink models to verify the combined behaviour of controllers and their respective plants [23–25]. The excitation signals are thereby derived using meta-heuristic search algorithms based on random search, adaptive random search, hill climbing or simulated annealing. The resulting output signals are then analysed with respect to specified signal properties.

A wide range of different methods and theories for hybrid verification was developed in [1]. This paper's approach to solve the problem is based on the well known concept of using system identification methods for verification as given in [21] which is extended to hybrid systems using the idea presented in [14].

In the engineering society diagnosis methods are used to monitor the correctness of running applications [11,17]. This is often done using "analytical redundancy" meaning that the real values of a process are compared to the expected values of the process [29]. The needed expected values are calculated using a model of the process and the measured input data.

The concept of analytical redundancy is transferred from monitoring to verification in this paper. The redundancy is thereby achieved by the identification of the dynamical system parameters from input/output data. This is possible because the generating system parameters describe the system behaviour exhaustively. The idea presented in this paper is to use the control engineering notation of hybrid systems and a recently developed hybrid identification procedure to verify complex hybrid systems. The continuous part of the hybrid system is thereby used to describe the system dynamics of the controlled plant. Note that the dynamics of the controlled plant are different from the genuine dynamics of the plant. This is due to the fact that the goal of the controller is to influence - and thus change - the genuine plant dynamics in a desired way. Furthermore note that it is hence not necessary to know or model the genuine dynamics of the plant. The discrete part of the hybrid system is predominantly used to describe the behaviour of the controller. Nevertheless the plant might contain switches in its continuous dynamics that are also modelled in the discrete part.

The necessary specification parameters have to be given directly by the user. The resulting parametrized system description can be used to reason about the consistency between specification and implementation. One advantage of this identification based method is the independence from specific input signals. This is due to the fact that different input/output pairs lead to the same parameters if they were generated using the same system dynamics.

The proposed method is introduced as follows: In Sect. 2 a formal specification consisting of a state machine and respective dynamical systems for each state is defined. Afterwards a method for the identification of data - measured using the SUT - is presented in Sect. 3. The identification can be interpreted as transformation of the SUT in a formal description. After the identification, the specification and the SUT are given in the same form. The automatic comparison is outlined in Sect. 4.

2   Formal Specification

Industrial specifications are often given in natural language or as a table containing a collection of more or less formal requirements [20]. Such a form is not suitable as basis for an automated verification algorithm. To allow the usage of automated methods a formal and strict notation has to be used for the specification. We focus on embedded systems consisting of a time, value and event discrete controller and a time and value continuous plant. We propose to model the resulting system as a hybrid system $\mathcal{H}$ according to Fig. 1. Thereby the embedded controller as well as the switching part of the physical plant are modelled using the state machine $\mathcal{Z}$. The controlled dynamics of the continuous plant are represented by a set of linear dynamic systems $\mathbb{S}$. The input u is applied to the state machine. Based on the resulting state, a switch signal is determined that activates the respective subsystem $s^{(i)} \in \mathbb{S}$. The continuous input is also applied to this continuous subsystem. The output of the active subsystem is fed to the output of the hybrid system and also used as feedback signal for the generating subsystem.

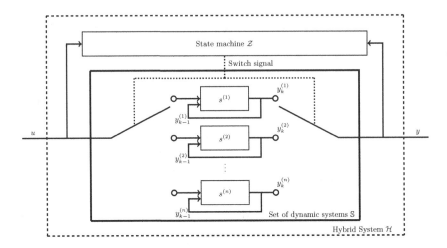

Fig. 1. Structure of the hybrid system model $\mathcal{H}$

Please note that this model assumption is different from the real system composition consisting of controller, actuator, plant and measurement device. This is due to the fact that the behaviour of the physical components is split into discrete and continuous dynamics and then combined in the respective model parts. Therefore it is not possible to use this detailed specification for any kind of automatic software generation. In other words, the hybrid system $\mathcal{H}$ represents *what* the system should do and not *how* it can be done. There is no information available whether a specific continuous dynamic $s^{(i)}$ is a genuine dynamic of the physical plant or if it is synthesised using a specific control strategy. This abstraction allows to describe the SUT by parameters calculated using identification methods, as the identified parameters uniquely describe the observed behaviour. Note that there are several possible combinations of (unknown) physical plant parameters and (unknown) controller parameters that will all show the same observable behaviour described by a unique set of parameters $\Theta^{(i)}$.

The state machine $\mathcal{Z}$ is assumed to be given by the 3-Tupel

$$\mathcal{Z} = (\mathbb{Q}, \mathbb{T}, q_0), \tag{1}$$

with a finite set of states $\mathbb{Q}$, a finite set of transitions $\mathbb{T}$, and an initial state q_0.

The state machine $\mathcal{Z}$ is used to describe the switching behaviour between distinctive states representing operation modes of the specification. Possible operation modes that are available in nearly all systems are for example "start up mode", "normal mode", "exception mode" or "shut down mode". Specific examples will provide even more, task specific operation modes.

The structure of the transitions $\mathbb{T}$ between the states $\mathbb{Q}$ of state machine $\mathcal{Z}$ is given by the adjacency matrix $\mathbf{A}$. With $a_{i,j} = 1$ if there exists a transition from state i to state j and $a_{i,j} = 0$ otherwise.

The linear dynamic subsystems $s^{(i)}$ for each state are defined as **Auto-Regressive** Systems with e**X**ogenous input (ARX system). All subsystems $s^{(i)}$

use the same fixed sample time ΔT. Each state $q^{(i)} \in \mathbb{Q}$ is linked to one specific dynamic ARX subsystem $s^{(i)} \in \mathbb{S}$ given by

$$s^{(i)} : \quad y_k = \sum_{j=1}^{n_a^{(i)}} (y_{k-j})\, a_j^{(i)} + \sum_{j=1}^{n_c^{(i)}} (u_{k-j})\, c_j^{(i)}, \tag{2}$$

were u_k and y_k are the values of the time discretized continuous system input and output at time k, $c_j^{(i)}$ and $a_j^{(i)}$ are the input and output coefficients and $n_c^{(i)}$ and $n_a^{(i)}$ are the input and output order, all specific for each subsystem.

Note that the specification parameters in $\mathbb{S}$ are parameters of the overall system (controller and plant) that describe the combined dynamics. Those parameters are different from the needed controller parameters and can thus not be used to parametrize the controller directly. The used controller structure as well as the controller parameters are an important part of the system design which is assumed to be done manually here. Please note that there are several controller structures and respective parametrizations that are suitable to meet the specification [26].

During the measurement time of $T = \Delta T K$ seconds the hybrid system shows the behaviour of the different active subsystems. Switches between the subsystems and thus the states of $\mathcal{Z}$ are often tightly coupled with conditions on the process. These conditions can be used to refine the state machine by the introduction of switching thresholds. The switching thresholds need to be fulfilled to allow the change of the active subsystem. Without switching thresholds, the state machine can switch between states at arbitrary values or after infinitely short dwell times, thus leading to undesired behaviour.

The switching thresholds are user-defined restrictions on a threshold signal $\Omega = [\omega_k]_{k=0}^K$ that can also be chosen by the user. The specified switching thresholds are given as interval entries of a matrix $\mathbf{B}$ with $b_{i,j} = [\underline{l}\ \bar{l}]$ if $a_{i,j} \neq 0$ and $b_{i,j} = [-\infty\ \infty]$ otherwise. Thereby are $\underline{l}$ and $\bar{l}$ lower and upper limits of the value of ω_k. As long as $\omega_k \in [\underline{l}\ \bar{l}]$ the state machine is allowed to change the state, i.e. to perform a switch, but not necessarily has to.

When setting up the formal specification the physical signals that are interpreted as input and output of the linear dynamic subsystem have to be chosen. The choice of the signals depends on the objective of the test and the investigated hierarchical level. It is possible to define specifications on different levels and thus map a variety of different goals. Nevertheless, the choice of the input signal $\mathbf{U} = [u_k]_{k=0}^K$ and the output signal $\mathbf{Y} = [y_k]_{k=0}^K$ of all subsystems and levels have to fulfil controllability constraints. The choice of the input and output signal has to be the same for all systems of $\mathbb{S}$.

To allow precise notation for the remainder of the paper, all variables of the formalized specification $\mathcal{H}^* = [\mathcal{Z}^*, \mathbb{S}^*]$ are marked with an asterisk. All variables belonging to the identified SUT $\mathcal{H}' = [\mathcal{Z}', \mathbb{S}']$ are marked with a dash. The complete setting is shown in Fig. 2. The specification $\mathcal{H}^*$, consisting of the state machine $\mathcal{Z}^*$ and the linear dynamic behaviour $\mathbb{S}^*$ has to be given by the user. Based on this information an SUT that fulfils the specification is

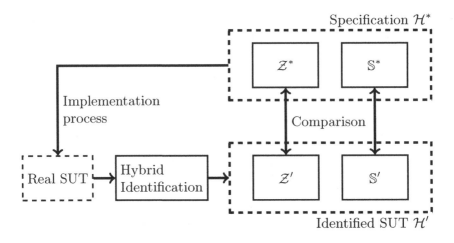

Fig. 2. Structure of the proposed method

developed. Nevertheless, it is likely that failures are made during the implementation process.

To verify the consistency, the SUT has to be transformed in its hybrid representation. A hybrid identification procedure is used to extract the implemented state machine $\mathcal{Z}'$ and the implemented system dynamics $\mathbb{S}'$ from the SUT. The final step is given by the comparison of the different system components as given in the previous section. If the correct subsystems are identified and the state machine is consistent with the specified state machine, the SUT is regarded as consistent with the given specification.

2.1 Example

To set up a formalized specification, the user has to define all elements of the 3-Tupel $\mathcal{Z}^*$ and all necessary parameters of the ARX systems included in $\mathbb{S}^*$. An exemplary specification $\mathcal{H}^* = [\mathcal{Z}^*, \mathbb{S}^*]$ is given by the system parameters in Table 1 and the state machine in Fig. 3. The state machine in the given example consists of three states and no switching thresholds for the sake of simplicity. The given system parameters describe three subsystems with $n_a^{(i)} = n_c^{(i)} = 1 \ \forall \ i$ leading to

$$s^{(i)} : \ y_k = y_{k-j}a_j^{(i)} + u_{k-j}c_j^{(i)}. \tag{3}$$

The implementation of the System under Test $\mathcal{H}'$ is done based on the given formal specification $\mathcal{H}^*$. As the implementation is done by one or more human developers, it is likely that there exist inconsistencies in the resulting system $\mathcal{H}'$. Note that the implemented system $\mathcal{H}'$ consists of real hard- and software and includes a given plant that can not be changed. Therefore the implemented state

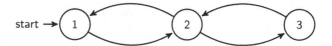

Fig. 3. Exemplary definition of the state machine $\mathcal{Z}^*$

Table 1. Exemplary parameters for the system $\mathbb{S}^*$ consisting of 3 subsystems with $n_a^{(i)} = n_c^{(i)} = 1 \forall i$

Subsystem	a_1^*	c_1^*
1	1,000	0,003
2	0,975	0,040
3	1,020	−0,040

machine $\mathcal{Z}'$ and its dynamical subsystems $\mathbb{S}'$ are not directly known. Nevertheless it is possible to excite the system and measure its output signal.

3   Identification of the SUT

Now assume the output signal of the system $\mathbf{Y}' = [y_k']_{k=0}^K$ was measured using a known, suitable and persistent excitation signal $\mathbf{U}' = [u_k']_{k=0}^K$ lasting for $T = \Delta TK$ seconds. It is now possible to calculate the actual generating subsystems $\mathbb{S}'$ based on the measured data $[\mathbf{U}', \mathbf{Y}']$ using the identification and segmentation algorithm from [14, 15] which is given as follows:

The algorithm uses an alternating iterative procedure to identify the system parameters as well as the unknown switching times. Thereby the system parameters are calculated using the first $\max(n_a^{(i)}, n_c^{(i)}) + n_a^{(i)} + n_c^{(i)}$ measurement values as estimation interval k_{est} and a Least-Squares-Estimator.

The estimated parameters

$$\mathbf{\Theta}'_{k_{est}} = \{\mathbf{a}^{(i)'}, \mathbf{c}^{(i)'}\} \tag{4}$$

with $\mathbf{a}^{(i)'} = \{a^{(i)'}\}_{j=0}^{n_a^{(i)}}$ and $\mathbf{c}^{(i)'} = \{c^{(i)'}\}_{j=0}^{n_c^{(i)}}$ are then used to determine the multi-step replica trajectory $\tilde{y}_k(\mathbf{\Theta}'_{k_{est}})$. As long as the calculated mean absolute error

$$\epsilon(k_{est}, \mathbf{\Theta}'_{k_{est}}) = \frac{1}{k_{est} + 1} \sum_{k=0}^{k_{est}} \left| y_k' - \tilde{y}_k(\mathbf{\Theta}'_{k_{est}}) \right| \tag{5}$$

is below a user defined border, the estimation interval k_{est} is increased. If $\epsilon(k_{est}, \mathbf{\Theta}'_{k_{est}})$ is bigger than the given border, a switch is recognized and the calculated parameters are stored as well as the current value $\omega_{k_{est}}$ of the threshold signal.

It is well known that only in a noiseless setting with known system orders, the estimation of the parameters yields a direct match with the specified parameters, even for short measurement times. Thus the switching time intervals shrink to a single point. This behaviour can be seen in Fig. 4 where the identification algorithm was applied to the output signal $\mathbf{Y}'$ generated by the system given in the example and a constant input signal $u_k = 100 \; \forall \; k$.

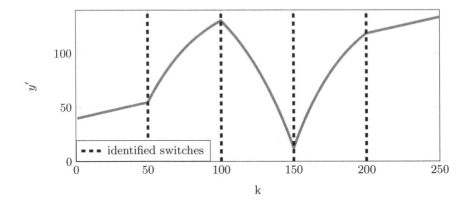

Fig. 4. Measured trajectory and identified subsystem switches

The resulting parameters of the subsystems are given in Table 2.

Table 2. Parameters identified from the signal given in Fig. 4

No	Subsystem	a_1'	c_1'
1	1	$1,000$	$0,003$
2	2	$0,975$	$0,040$
3	3	$1,020$	$-0,040$
4	2	$0,975$	$0,040$
5	1	$1,000$	$0,003$

4 Comparison of SUT and Specification

The results can now be compared with the given specification $\mathcal{H}^*$. Matching parameters mean that the dynamic behaviour of $\mathbb{S}'$ is consistent with the specified behaviour $\mathbb{S}^*$. Manual inspection shows that the identified parameters in Table 2 match the specified parameters in Table 1. The identified state sequence of the signal in Fig. 4 is $1 \rightarrow 2 \rightarrow 3 \rightarrow 2 \rightarrow 1$ which is consistent with the state machine in Fig. 3. Therefore it can be concluded that the system that produced the signal in Fig. 4 is consistent with the given specification $\mathcal{H}^*$.

4.1 Automatic Comparison

The comparison of the specification $\mathcal{H}^*$ and the SUT $\mathcal{H}'$ can also be done automatically. Therefore it is necessary to check the consistency of the parameters, the consistency of the transitions and the consistency of the switching thresholds. There are three possible results: *full consistency*, *partial consistency* and *inconsistency* for each part.

The consistency of the parameters is determined by setting up the identified set of states $\mathbb{Q}'$. This is done by comparing the identified parameters to the specified parameters. An identified subsystem $s^{(i)'}$ can be assigned to a specified state $q_j \in \mathbb{Q}^*$ if the parameters of $s^{(i)'}$ and $s^{(j)^*}$ are the same. The matching state q_j is added to the identified set of states $\mathbb{Q}'$. An identified subsystem $s^{(i)'}$ without a matching specification is considered to represent an additional dynamic belonging to a state $q_m \notin \mathbb{Q}^*$. Nevertheless q_m is added to $\mathbb{Q}'$.

The consistency can be determined by comparing $\mathbb{Q}^*$ and $\mathbb{Q}'$. The set of states is only *fully consistent* if $\mathbb{Q}' = \mathbb{Q}^*$. If there are states missing and hence $\mathbb{Q}' \subset \mathbb{Q}^*$ the states are *partially consistent*. Otherwise they are *inconsistent* as $\mathbb{Q}' \not\subset \mathbb{Q}^*$ indicates that there are unspecified dynamics present in the SUT.

The consistency of the transitions is determined by comparing the adjacency matrices of the specification $\mathbf{A}^* \in \mathbb{R}^{e \times e}$ and the SUT $\mathbf{A}' \in \mathbb{R}^{f \times f}$. Therefore it is necessary to reorder the identified states such that they match the order of the specified states. Each specified system dynamic without an identified match leads to zero entries in $\mathbf{A}'$, each unspecified system dynamic leads to an additional row and an additional column in $\mathbf{A}'$.

For *full consistency* between $\mathbf{A}^*$ and $\mathbf{A}'$ has to hold:

$$\mathbf{A}^* = \mathbf{A}'. \tag{6}$$

Meaning that exactly all specified states and all transitions were identified, no state or transition is missing and no additional state or transition was present.

For *partial consistency* between $\mathbf{A}^*$ and $\mathbf{A}'$ has to hold:

$$e = f \tag{7}$$
$$\underline{0} \preccurlyeq \mathbf{A}^* - \mathbf{A}' \tag{8}$$

with $\mathbf{A} \succcurlyeq \underline{0}$ meaning $a_{ij} \geq 0 \ \forall \ i,j$. *Partial consistency* means that all identified states and transitions were specified but not all specified states and transitions were identified. This is due to the fact that any specified system dynamic without an identified match leads to zero entries in $\mathbf{A}'$. Nevertheless the system might possess *full consistency* but did not show it due to insufficient excitation.

There is *inconsistency* between $\mathbf{A}^*$ and $\mathbf{A}'$ if:

$$e = f \tag{9}$$
$$\underline{0} \not\preccurlyeq \mathbf{A}^* - \mathbf{A}' \tag{10}$$

or

$$e \neq f. \tag{11}$$

The adjacency matrices $\mathbf{A}^*$ and $\mathbf{A}'$ are of different dimension if there are additional states that are not specified. Unspecified behaviour leads to additional states and thus an additional row and an additional column in $\mathbf{A}'$. If there are no unspecified states but unspecified transitions present (9) and (10) hold. As soon as there are unspecified states or transitions present, the transitions are *inconsistent* with the specification.

For the switching thresholds given in $\mathbf{B}^*$ the consistency has to be checked for all identified transitions $\mathbb{T}'$. Therefore the relevant signals have to fulfil

$$\omega_{\tau_{i,j}} \in b_{i,j} \ \forall \ \mathbb{T}' \tag{12}$$

with $\tau_{i,j}$ denoting the time when the active state of the state machine changes from state i to state j. The switching thresholds are *inconsistent* if (12) does not hold. Otherwise they are *partially consistent* for $\mathbb{T}' \subset \mathbb{T}^*$ and *fully consistent* for $\mathbb{T}' = \mathbb{T}^*$.

The final consistency of $\mathcal{H}'$ is determined by the combination of the result for all three parts as given in Table 3.

Table 3. Consistency of $\mathcal{H}'$

Consistency of			
$\mathbb{Q}'$	$\mathbf{A}'$	$\mathbb{T}'$	$\mathcal{H}'$
fully	*fully*	*fully*	*fully*
partially	*fully/partially*	*fully/partially*	*partially*
fully/partially	*partially*	*fully/partially*	
fully/partially	*fully/partially*	*partially*	
inconsistent	*any*	*any*	*inconsistent*
any	*inconsistent*	*any*	
any	*any*	*inconsistent*	

Thereby $\mathcal{H}'$ is only *fully consistent* if all results were *fully consistent*. If there are *fully* and *partially consistent* results, $\mathcal{H}'$ is *partially consistent*. Finally $\mathcal{H}'$ becomes *inconsistent* with $\mathcal{H}^*$ if there is at least one part evaluated as *inconsistent*.

4.2   Example

The states in the example are given by

$$\mathbb{Q}' = \{1, 2, 3\} = \mathbb{Q}^* \tag{13}$$

and are thus *fully consistent*. The adjacency matrices are given by

$$\mathbf{A'} = \begin{bmatrix} 0 & 1 & 0 \\ 1 & 0 & 1 \\ 0 & 1 & 0 \end{bmatrix} = \mathbf{A}^* \tag{14}$$

and are thus also *fully consistent*. As there are no switching thresholds defined, this part can be omitted. This leads to $\mathcal{Z}'$ being *fully consistent* with $\mathcal{Z}^*$ and in addition $\mathbb{S}'$ being *fully consistent* with $\mathbb{S}^*$ leading to $\mathcal{H}'$ being *fully consistent* with $\mathcal{H}^*$. Which means that the superimposed state machine as well as the linear dynamic subsystems of the system that produced the measurement in Fig. 4 are *fully consistent* with the specification of $\mathcal{H}^*$ in Fig. 3 and Table 1.

5 Conclusions and Future Work

5.1 Conclusions

This paper presented the idea of interpreting an automated verification of complex systems task as an identification of hybrid systems setting. Therefore the idea of using a formal hybrid model as specification for the complex system was presented. Each operation mode of the specification is interpreted as state of a state machine. The continuous linear system dynamics that govern the behaviour in every state are modelled as ARX systems and assigned to the respective state. Representing system behaviour as dynamic parameters leads to the advantage of being independent from specific input/output signals.

Knowledge about the implemented SUT is generated by exciting the SUT with a suitable input signal and measuring the resulting output signal. This signal can be generated by the responsible engineer and thus provides the possibility to include expert knowledge in the verification process. The measurement data is analysed by a hybrid identification algorithm that segments and identifies a hybrid system from its input/output behaviour. The resulting system parameters are then compared with the specified parameters. Based on the result, the state machine of the SUT can be set up. If the identified parameters and the identified state machine are consistent with the specification it can be concluded that the SUT itself is consistent with its specification.

5.2 Future Work

The requirement that the user has to define all elements of the 3-Tupel and all necessary parameters of the ARX-System when setting up the formalized specification is rather restricting. This should be improved in future work by providing a more intuitive way of setting up the specification. Therefore a graphical user interface (GUI) can be implemented, providing the user with the ability to define feasible input regions that are linked to their respective feasible output region. The specification parameters could hence be determined by the improved algorithm, based on this user specified input/output trajectories leading to a "specification by example" setting.

The restrictions on the choice of the input and output signal given in Sect. 2 are rather rigorous. Future work will focus on softening these restrictions to allow a wider scope of application.

Furthermore the impact of noise has to be investigated. It is clear that the identified parameters will not perfectly match the specified parameters any more if there is noise present. The general procedure is assumed to be still applicable as [14] already provides the handling of noisy signals. Nevertheless it is not enough to simply introduce tolerances for the parameters, as even minor changes in the parameters might lead to tremendous changes of the system behaviour in some scenarios. On the other hand system identification can provide two distinct sets of parameters even though the input/output behaviour is very similar. Both cases have to be tackled by the introduction of a similarity measure based on the parameters.

References

1. Transregional collaborative research center "automatic verification and analysis of complex systems (avacs)". http://www.avacs.org
2. Abel, A., Reineke, J.: Memin: sat-based exact minimization of incompletely specified mealy machines. In: Proceedings of the IEEE/ACM International Conference on Computer-Aided Design, ICCAD 2015, Austin, TX, USA, 2–6 November 2015, pp. 94–101 (2015)
3. Alur, R., Dang, T., Ivančić, F.: Reachability analysis of hybrid systems via predicate abstraction. In: Tomlin, C.J., Greenstreet, M.R. (eds.) HSCC 2002. LNCS, vol. 2289, pp. 35–48. Springer, Heidelberg (2002). doi:10.1007/3-540-45873-5_6
4. Alur, R., Dang, T., Ivančić, F.: Predicate abstraction for reachability analysis of hybrid systems. ACM Trans. Embed. Comput. Syst. 5(1), 152–199 (2006)
5. Anta, A., Majumdar, R., Saha, I., Tabuada, P.: Automatic verification of control system implementations. In: Proceedings of the Tenth ACM International Conference on Embedded Software, pp. 9–18 (2010)
6. Araiza-Illan, D., Eder, K., Richards, A.: Verification of control systems implemented in simulink with assertion checks and theorem proving: a case study. In: 2015 European Control Conference (ECC), pp. 2670–2675, July 2015
7. Badban, B., Fränzle, M., Peleska, J., Teige, T.: Test automation for hybrid systems. In: Proceedings of the 3rd International Workshop on Software Quality Assurance, SOQUA 2006, pp. 14–21. ACM, New York (2006)
8. Balluchi, A., Benvenuti, L., di Benedetto, M.D., Pinello, C., Sangiovanni-Vincentelli, A.L.: Automotive engine control and hybrid systems: challenges and opportunities. Proc. IEEE 88(7), 888–912 (2000)
9. Bhatia, A., Frazzoli, E.: Incremental search methods for reachability analysis of continuous and hybrid systems. In: Alur, R., Pappas, G. (eds.) HSCC 2004. LNCS, vol. 2993, pp. 142–156. Springer, Berlin Heidelberg (2004)
10. Broy, M., Jonsson, B., Katoen, J.-P., Leucker, M., Pretschner, A. (eds.): Model-Based Testing of Reactive Systems: Advanced Lectures. LNCS, vol. 3472. Springer, Heidelberg (2005)
11. Chen, W., Chen, W.-T., Saif, M., Li, M.-F., Wu, H.: Simultaneous fault isolation and estimation of lithium-ion batteries via synthesized design of luenberger and learning observers. IEEE Trans. Control Syst. Technol. 22(1), 290–298 (2014)

12. Dang, T.: Model-based testing of hybrid systems. In: Model-Based Testing for Embedded Systems, chap. 14, pp. 383–424

13. Denise, A., Gaudel, M.-C., Gouraud, S.-D.: A generic method for statistical testing. In: 15th International Symposium on Software Reliability Engineering, ISSRE 2004, pp. 25–34 (2004)

14. Diehm, G., Maier, S., Flad, M., Hohmann, S.: An identification method for individual driver steering behaviour modelled by switched affine systems. In: Proceedings of the 52nd IEEE Conference on Decision and Control, pp. 3547–3553 (2013)

15. Diehm, G., Maier, S., Flad, M., Hohmann, S.: Online identification of individual driver steering behaviour and experimental results. In: Proceedings of the IEEE International Conference on Systems, Man and Cybernetics, pp. 221–227 (2013)

16. Föllinger, O., Konigorski, U.: Regelungstechnik: Einführung die Methoden und ihre Anwendung, 11, völlig neu bearb. aufl. edn. VDE-Verl., Berlin (2013)

17. Frank, P.M.: Diagnoseverfahren in der Automatisierungstechnik. at - Automatisierungstechnik, 47–64 (1994)

18. Holling, D., Pretschner, A., Gemmar, M.: 8cage: lightweight fault-based test generation for simulink. In: Proceedings of the 29th ACM/IEEE International Conference on Automated Software Engineering, ASE 2014, pages 859–862. ACM, New York (2014)

19. Kaner, C.: An introduction to scenario testing (2003)

20. Lin, L., Poore, J.H., Eschbach, R., Hierons, R.M., Robinson-Mallett, C.: Augmenting sequence enumeration with string-rewriting for requirements analysis and behavioral specification. In: Cortellessa, V., Varró, D. (eds.) FASE 2013. LNCS, vol. 7793, pp. 179–193. Springer, Heidelberg (2013). doi:10.1007/978-3-642-37057-1_13

21. Liu, D., Guo, X., Tang, G., Huang, Z.: Model Validation via System Identification and Hypothesis Test. Springer, Heidelberg (2012)

22. Maler, O., Nickovic, D.: Monitoring temporal properties of continuous signals. In: Lakhnech, Y., Yovine, S. (eds.) FORMATS/FTRTFT-2004. LNCS, vol. 3253, pp. 152–166. Springer, Heidelberg (2004). doi:10.1007/978-3-540-30206-3_12

23. Matinnejad, R., Nejati, S., Briand, L., Bruckmann, T., Poull, C.: Proceedings of the 5th International Symposium on Search based software engineering, SSBSE 2013, St. Petersburg, Russia, 24–26 August 2013, pp. 141–157 (2013)

24. Matinnejad, R., Nejati, S., Briand, L., Bruckmann, T., Poull, C.: Search-based automated testing of continuous controllers: framework, tool support, and case studies. Inf. Softw. Technol. **57**, 705–722 (2015)

25. Matinnejad, R., Nejati, S., Briand, L.C., Bruckmann, T.: Automated test suite generation for time-continuous simulink models, pp. 595–606 (2016)

26. Pajic, M., Park, J., Lee, I., Pappas, G.J., Sokolsky, O.: Automatic verification of linear controller software. In: Proceedings of the 12th International Conference on Embedded Software, EMSOFT 2015, pp. 217–226. IEEE Press, Piscataway (2015)

27. Schneider, J.: Tracking down root causes of defects in simulink models. In: Proceedings of the 29th ACM/IEEE International Conference on Automated Software Engineering, ASE 2014, pp. 599–604. ACM, New York (2014)

28. Schupp, S., Ábrahám, E., Chen, X., Makhlouf, I., Frehse, G., Sankaranarayanan, S., Kowalewski, S.: Current challenges in the verification of hybrid systems. In: Berger, C., Mousavi, M.R. (eds.) CyPhy 2015. LNCS, vol. 9361, pp. 8–24. Springer, Heidelberg (2015). doi:10.1007/978-3-319-25141-7_2

29. Simon, S.: Objektorientierte Methoden zum automatisierten Entwurf von modellbasierten Diagnosesystemen. PhD thesis, Berlin, 2015. Zugl.: Kaiserslautern, Techn. Univ., Diss. (2015)

30. Utting, M., Pretschner, A., Legeard, B.: A taxonomy of model-based testing (2006)
31. Yordanov, B., Belta, C.: Formal analysis of discrete-time piecewise affine systems. IEEE Trans. Autom. Control **55**(12), 2834–2840 (2010)
32. Zander-Nowicka, J.: Model-based testing of real-time embedded systems in the automotive domain (2009)
33. Zhao, F., Koutsoukos, X., Haussecker, H., Reich, J., Cheung, P.: Monitoring and fault diagnosis of hybrid systems. IEEE Trans. Syst. Man Cybern. Part B (Cybern.) **35**(6), 1225–1240 (2005)

Ontological Reasoning as an Enabler of Contract-Based Co-design

Ken Vanherpen[1,3(✉)], Joachim Denil[1,2,3], Paul De Meulenaere[1,3], and Hans Vangheluwe[2,3,4]

[1] CoSys-Lab (FTI), University of Antwerp, Antwerp, Belgium
{ken.vanherpen,joachim.denil,paul.demeulenaere}@uantwerp.be
[2] AnSyMo (FWET), University of Antwerp, Antwerp, Belgium
[3] Flanders Make vzw, Lommel, Belgium
[4] MSDL, McGill University, Montréal, QC, Canada
hv@cs.mcgill.ca

Abstract. Because of the combination of computational, networking and physical artifacts, different engineering disciplines are involved in the design of a Cyber-Physical System (CPS). This multidisciplinary approach leads to different, often contradicting, views on the system under design which in the end might lead to inconsistencies between domain specific properties. Contract-Based Design (CBD) aims to prevent these contradictions by defining possible conflicting properties in a contract. These contracts consist of a set of pre- and postconditions.

Although the current state-of-the-art describes the abstraction/ refinement, composition and multi-view analysis and verification principles of CBD, it lacks methods and techniques to identify the shared properties in concurrent design processes. By combining the theory of CBD with the principles of ontological reasoning, this paper intents to provide a framework which enables Contract-Based Co-Design (CBCD). The feasibility of this framework will be explained by means of a running CPS example.

Keywords: Co-design · Contract-based design · Cyber-physical systems · Ontological reasoning · Ontologies

1 Introduction

Increasingly more, Cyber-Physical Systems (CPS) [1,2] take a prominent role in a wide range of application areas such as transportation, manufacturing, health care, etc. They extend traditional mechanical systems with computational and networking capabilities making (daily life) products smarter, faster, more accurate, remotely controllable, and so forth. Therefore, CPS are considered as one of the key enablers of the fourth industrial revolution.

Despite the extended capabilities of CPS, its development process is characterized by costly, iterative, design cycles partly due to the involvement of various

© Springer International Publishing AG 2017
C. Berger et al. (Eds.): CyPhy 2016, LNCS 10107, pp. 101–115, 2017.
DOI: 10.1007/978-3-319-51738-4_8

engineering disciplines, each with a different view and set of concerns of the system under design [3]. The involvement of these different stakeholders can lead to inconsistencies between shared properties, causing unexpected behaviors during the integration of the different design artifacts. To preserve consistency between those different views, Contract-Based Design (CBD) [4–6] is increasingly being used by system engineers to formalize an agreement between two or more engineering domains. Originating from contracts used in software engineering, such an agreement consists out of a set of assumptions and guarantees. These assumptions and guarantees describe the conditions under which a system promises to operate while satisfying desired properties.

Given the increasing complexity of Cyber-Physical Systems, aggravated by the need for cost-efficient products and shorter development time, the need for concurrent design (co-design) processes arises. Concurrent design makes engineers reason about common design properties to allow the independent development of parts of the system. In that sense, Contract-Based Design seems to be a useful methodology. Different contributions have been made elaborating on abstraction/refinement, verification and validation of contracts (see Sect. 2).

However, the current state-of-the-art does not allow the engineers to reason about the content of such a contract. It thus lacks in its applicability to the co-design of Cyber-Physical Systems. This paper intents to provide a framework which enables Contract-Based Co-Design (CBCD) by combining the current state-of-the-art of CBD with the principles of ontological reasoning [7]. The latter enables one to make the implicit knowledge of each engineer explicit by using ontological properties and certain influence relationships between them.

The rest of this paper is structured as follows. Section 2 gives an overview of the related work. The running CPS example is introduced in Sect. 3, while an overview of the currently used contract operators is given in Sect. 4. Similar to the proposed methodology in the current state-of-the-art, Sect. 5 investigates the applicability of the current theory in a co-design engineering process. However, some shortcomings will emerge which are resolved by our proposed CBCD methodology in Sect. 6. Finally, Sect. 7 concludes our contribution and gives an overview of our future work.

2   Related Work

Contract-Based Design finds its origin in the late 80's when Bertrand Meyer introduced the Eiffel programming language to enable contract-based software development [8,9]. Eiffel introduces *Require* and *Ensure* clauses that correspond to respectively a set of pre- and post-conditions under which a software routine ensures to operates.

More than a decade later, the use of contracts during the design of CPS came to the attention of some researchers, including Damm [10,11]. He introduced the concept of 'rich components' to deal with uncertainty when designing Cyber-Physical Systems. Rich components extend model components such that: (a) they cover all the specifications of the involved viewpoints, (b) they contain a set of assumptions and guarantees with respect to the context of the component, and (c) they provide classifiers to the assumptions.

In the framework of the European project SPEEDS[1], the work of Damm was extended by Josko et al. [12] and Benvenuti et al. [13] by means of 'Heterogeneous Rich Component' (HRC) which supports the integration of heterogeneous viewpoints on a system with different semantics originating from multiple design layers and tools. Therefore, a common meta-model was developed in [14]. Similar but less comprehensive approaches, however, were already introduced by the MARTE UML profile [15] and as a modelling framework called Metropolis [16]. The scope of the SPEEDS project resulted in the (first) use of contracts in a component based engineering context. In [17], Benveniste et al. present the mathematical foundations of CBD to enable the combination of contracts for different model components and the combination of contracts for different viewpoints on the same model component. According to the authors, a contract as such consists out of a pair of *Assumptions* and *Guarantees* formulated as $C = (A, G)$. Note that this relates to the *Require* and *Ensure* clauses introduced by Meyer [9].

In the scope of the European project CESAR[2], Benveniste et al. extended their theory and showed how contracts might be used through multiple application cases [4,18]. They show that there exist three fundamental contract operators to combine contracts: refinement, composition and conjunction [4,19].

Based on the work of Benveniste et al., Graf et al. describe how circular and non-circular assume-guarantee reasoning can be used in order to check for contract dominance [20]. They make use of two frameworks, L0 and L1, which are focused on component refinement and component interactions respectively.

Sangiovanni-Vincentelli et al. address the emergent need of CBD in the context of system level design [6]. They present a design methodology that combines the concepts of CBD with Platform-Based Design (PBD) as a meet-in-the-middle approach. Related to the work of Graf et al. [20], Sangiovanni-Vincentelli et al. demonstrate how contracts may be dominated when combining subsystems (individually bounded by a contract). Furthermore, a clear distinction is made between horizontal and vertical contracts when combining the concepts of CBD with PBD. Similarly, Nuzzo et al. elaborate on the usefulness of CBD, and their formal analysis and verification methods, in a PBD methodology for Cyber-Physical Systems [21,22]. Besides going into detail on the different methods and tools that are used to enable their methodology, an aircraft electric power distribution system is used as a demonstrator.

In [5], a more general framework of design contracts in the context of CPS design is given. Derler et al. focus on timing properties to facilitate the communication between control and embedded engineers. A non-exhaustive enumeration of contract types is given each with a specific set of parameters having a common interest to both engineering domains. Depending on the type of contract

---

[1] www.speeds.eu.com.

[2] http://www.cesarproject.eu.

(and therefore the formalized set of parameters), an actual implementation of the contract is feasible for one or both of the engineering domains.

Törngren et al. describe the different viewpoints involved in the design of a mechatronic system [3]. Furthermore, they show how these viewpoints are interrelated by means of supporting models at different design levels, namely: (a) people level, (b) models level and (c) tools level. At each design level, some challenges and solutions (supporting models) are described. For the contributions of our work, the first two levels are particularly interesting. At people level, the authors point out that each stakeholder, involved in the design of a CPS, should be aware of the effect of his/her work on others. To enable this, the use of design contracts, as suggested by Derler et al. [5], is proposed. Moreover, they hint towards the use of assumptions and guarantees as discussed by [6]. Additionally, at models level, Törngren et al. describe the existence of dependencies between models implementing certain parts of the overall system requirements.

We conclude this section with the work of Persson et al. where the authors characterize model-based approaches used in the design of Cyber-Physical Systems [23]. To do so, a clear distinction is made between *views* and *viewpoints*. The former relates to the multitude of abstractions that can be made of a system while the latter refers to a set of all possible view instances. The authors show that there exist relations between views, and as such viewpoints, with respect to their content, process and operations which are not entirely exclusive to each other. This is illustrated by an academic case study of a wind-shield wiper system.

3   The Power Window as a Running Example

To clarify the current state-of-the-art in Sect. 5 and to detail our contribution in Sect. 6, we use the power window as a running example.

As every system, the power window is specified by a set of requirements. These requirements describe the expected behavior of the system given a certain context. Given that the power window system operates in a vehicle, we describe the most elementary behavior of the power window as follows [24]:

1. The power window should start moving within 200 ms after a command is issued.
2. The power window shall be fully opened or closed within 4.5 s.
3. When closing the power window, a force of no more than 100 N may be present.
4. Detection of a clamped object when closing the window should lower the window by 10 cm.

Given these requirements, the power window system can be seen as a black box controller with three inputs and two outputs as illustrated in Fig. 1.

Using the definition of contracts for system design from [4,19], the set of requirements are formalized as a system contract,

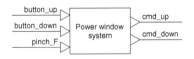

Fig. 1. Representation of the power window system

as shown in Table 1. The contract specifies certain assumptions on the context/environment the power window operates in, namely: (a) the input force is lower than 1000 N and (b) the minimum interval of button operations is 100 ms. Under these conditions, a safe operation of the system is guaranteed. It might be clear that the requirements of the system are the guarantees of the system. However, as one may notice in Table 1, certain functional requirements are refined given domain-specific knowledge. For example, requirement *3* and *4* are further refined in the spatial and temporal dimension to detail the safety requirement:

1. Spatial dimension: if a clamped object is detected, the power window may continue to close for a maximum of 0.2 mm before life threatening injuries occur.
2. Temporal dimension: given the spatial dimensions, safety can be guaranteed if the window lowers within 1 ms.

This refinement, that is made after discussions with experts and looking into regulations, results in the fifth guarantee of Table 1.

Table 1. Power window system contract Csys

Assumptions	*pinch_F* will be lower than 1000 N
	button_up occurs sporadic with a minimum period of 100 ms
	button_down occurs sporadic with a minimum period of 100 ms
Guarantees	Delay between *button_up* and *cmd_up* within [0 ms, 200 ms]
	Delay between *button_down* and *cmd_down* within [0 ms, 200 ms]
	Maximum activation time *cmd_up* within [0 ms, 4.5 s]
	Maximum activation time *cmd_down* within [0 ms, 4.5 s]
	If *pinch_F* exceeds 100 N, delay between *pinch_F* and *cmd_down* within [0 ms, 1 ms]
	If *pinch_F* exceeds 100 N, activation time *cmd_down* within [0 s, 0.43 s]

4 Overview of the State-of-the-Art Contract Operators

In Sect. 2 it is shown that a lot of contributions in the field of Contract-Based Design for Cyber-Physical Systems have been done in the context of the SPEEDS and CESAR projects. Therefore, this section gives a short overview of the currently used contract operators. Section 5 uses these operators to check their feasibility in a co-design engineering process.

Decomposition of a System

Concurrent engineering (co-design) can be realized by decomposing the system into components that are designed (semi-)independently of each other. From the perspective of a CPS, one can distinguish three independent components: (a) a hardware component, i.e. one or more embedded platforms which are connected to each other, (b) a control component and (c) a mechanical component. Each component is typed by a set of in- and outputs, a set of behaviors and a set of extra-functional properties like performance, timing, energy, safety, etc. Figure 2 shows the *decomposition* of the power window system (Fig. 1) into its control and hardware component. Note that we neglected the mechanical component for the sake of clarity. As can be seen, components can be further *refined* and hierarchically structured to represent different levels of *abstraction*. They can be connected to each other by sharing certain ports and variables.

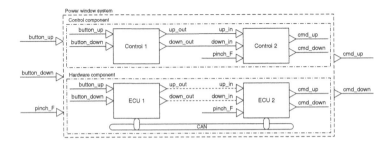

Fig. 2. Refinement of the power window system

The decomposition of the system results in a decomposition of the system contract as well. Indeed, each (sub-)component is typed by an individual contract that is derived from the system contract. By using different operators, the component contracts are merged and should satisfy or refine the system contract.

Contract Operators. Because a contract is a set of assumptions and guarantees, set theory is used to merge component contracts. Three basic operators are defined in literature [19]: abstraction/refinement $\preceq$, conjunction $\wedge$ and composition $\otimes$. Before applying the current CBD theory to our example, we briefly discuss these basic operators.

Abstraction/Refinement. As already stated, components might be hierarchical structured and as such, a component its contract might be further refined. Let $C' = (A', G')$ and $C = (A, G)$ be two contracts consisting out of a set of assumptions and guarantees. The refinement $C' \preceq C$ holds if and only if:

$$A' \supseteq A$$
$$G' \subseteq G$$

(1)

Given this constraint, it is clear that a refined contract should weaken the assumptions and strengthen the guarantees. Therefore, we say that any implementation M of contract C' is an implementation of C as well, or more formally:

$$\text{If } M \models C' \text{ and } C' \preceq C \text{ then } M \models C \qquad (2)$$

A similar reasoning can be obtained for the environment E of both contracts:

$$\text{If } E \models C \text{ and } C' \preceq C \text{ then } E \models C' \qquad (3)$$

Conjunction. The conjunction operators enables one the merge different viewpoint contracts associated to one single component. In the example of Fig. 2, the component 'Control 1' might be typed by a behavioral and a safety viewpoint contract. Let $C_1 = (A_1, G_1)$ and $C_2 = (A_2, G_2)$ be two viewpoint contracts consisting out of a set of assumptions and guarantees. The conjunction $C_1 \wedge C_2$ can then be obtained as follows:

$$
\begin{aligned}
A &= (A_1 \cup A_2) \\
G &= (G_1 \cap G_2)
\end{aligned}
\qquad (4)
$$

Similar to the abstraction/refinement operator, the conjunction operator weakens the assumptions and strengthens the guarantees.

Composition. The composition operator enables one to merge the contracts associated to different components. In the example of Fig. 2, the contracts related to the sub-components 'Control 1' and 'Control 2' can be composed to compute the 'Control' contract. Let $C_1 = (A_1, G_1)$ and $C_2 = (A_2, G_2)$ be two components contracts consisting out of a set of assumptions and guarantees. The composition $C_1 \otimes C_2$ can then be obtained as follows:

$$
\begin{aligned}
A &= (A_1 \cap A_2) \cup \neg (G_1 \cap G_2) \\
G &= (G_1 \cap G_2)
\end{aligned}
\qquad (5)
$$

In the case of composition, both assumptions and guarantees are strengthened.

5 Applicability of the Current Methodologies on a Co-Design Engineering Problem

To the best of our knowledge, the current CBD theory has never been applied in a co-design engineering process. On the contrary, the examples shown in [4,21,22] are sequential engineering processes. Therefore, this section analyzes the feasibility of the current state-of-the-art/state-of-the-practice and identifies possible shortcomings using the power window example of Sect. 3.

Control Component

As can be seen in Fig. 2, the control component is decomposed into two control components. One component takes care of the user operations (button up and button down) and as such implements guarantee 1 and 2 of the system contract of Table 1. The other control component implements the main control loop which takes care of the remaining guarantees.

The composition of the two refined control components refines (the control view of) the system contract of Table 1 and will, using Eq. 1, strengthen (some) guarantees and weaken (some) assumptions. As an example, Table 2 shows a fragment of the contract of component 'Control 1' which is obtained by the conjunction of its functional and timing contract and the composition with the signal contract. The later one specifies a contract on the signals between 'Control 1' and 'Control 2'. The refined contract strengthens the guarantees of the system contract. In 'control 1' the delay between the component its input and its output (in fact, the input of the other component) is lowered from 200 ms to 52 ms. Together with the contract of 'Control 2', the total time is less than 200 ms. Furthermore, Eq. 3 holds because the environment of the composed refined components will be one for the system as well. Note that the actual refinement of the system contract is the conjunction of the composition of the hardware components and the composition of the control components.

Table 2. Fragment of contract Cc1 for 'Control 1'

Assumptions	*button_up* occurs sporadic with a minimum period of 50 ms
	up_out occurs sporadic with a minimum period of 2 ms
Guarantees	Delay between *button_up* and *up_in* within $[0\,ms, 52\,ms]$

If we take a closer look at the content of the contract in Table 2, we may wonder to what extent a control engineer is able to guarantee these timing delays. Although a control engineer has several degrees of freedom (e.g. the order of the control algorithm) to influence the computational expensiveness of a algorithm, these timings highly depend on the hardware platform and thus on the hardware component. From our experience with industry, we know that control engineers have limited aids in estimating hardware properties and as such are not able to guarantee these delays once the control algorithm is deployed.

Hardware Component

A similar conclusion can be made when looking to the contract for the hardware component, and in particular for the contract of 'ECU 1' (see fragment in Table 3) which implements the algorithm of 'Control 1'. Note that the composition of this contract with the 'ECU 2' and 'CAN' contract is again a refinement of the (hardware view of the) system contract, which one can verify using Eqs. 1–3.

At a first glance, the contract contains everything an embedded engineer is able to reason about: timing period of a runnable, Worst Case Execution Time

Table 3. Fragment of contract Ce1 for 'ECU 1'

Assumptions	*button_up* occurs sporadic with a minimum period of 40 ms
	Runnable#actuation occurs each 40 ms
	Delay between *Runnable#actuation* and *up_out* within [0 ms, 10 ms]
Guarantees	Timer occurs each 10 ms
	Delay between *button_up* and *up_out* within [200 us, 10 ms + 1.3 ms]

(WCET) and Worst Case Response Time (WRT). However, their position in the table is questionable. To be more specific, both parts of the table reason about these properties, while they should be clear guarantees of the platform.

Shortcomings

From this example, we conclude that the current state-of-the-art does not support a co-design process because the individual contracts: (a) contain properties on which the domain engineer lacks the ability to reason about and/or (b) make no clear separation between what is assumed from the other domain and what should be guaranteed under these conditions.

6   A Contract-Based Co-design Methodology

To overcome the aforementioned shortcomings, a clear negotiation phase is included in the proposed engineering process. This results in a so called mapping contract. Based on this overall contract, the different domain-specific contracts are derived and further refined. This process for deriving domain-specific contracts from a negotiated contract was already suggested by Derler et al. in [5]. However, a clear methodology was not proposed. Therefore, we suggest to use domain ontologies to support this Contract-Based Design process.

In its essence, an ontology is typed by a set of ontological properties and certain influence relationships which exists between those properties. Each ontological property classifies a certain part of the real world.

In the context of Cyber-Physical Systems, ontologies are ideal to make the implicit knowledge of each domain engineer explicit. Based on our earlier work [7], Fig. 3 shows a formal representation of ontological reasoning in a CPS design context. Given a set of requirements, which describes the real-world system for a certain context, the engineer reasons about certain domain properties (which might be related to each other). The solid oval in the *Ontological World* denotes the set of ontological properties covered by the requirements.

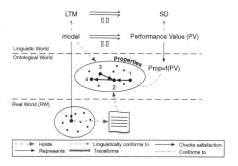

Fig. 3. Ontological reasoning

As a first step in the design process, the engineer abstracts the real-world system by means of a model. This model is typed by a meta-model, called a *Linguistic Type Model* (*LTM*). A linguistic conformance relationship exists between the model and the LTM. By transforming the model to a *Semantic Domain* (*SD*), using a semantic mapping function ([[.]]), a meaning is given to the model. This allows for analysis of linguistic properties which are called *Performance Values* (*PV*). The engineer evaluates these performance values to his own implicit knowledge of the system. This allows the engineer to conclude whether the system is conforming to the requirements or not.

By making this knowledge explicit using an ontology, a function returning a logical value can be used to evaluate these performance values against a certain ontological property. As discussed in [7], ontological reasoning enables us to reason about consistency between performance values related to different ontological properties. These properties in turn are connected by means of influence relationships.

We argue that ontological reasoning enables contract-based co-design of a CPS. Given the requirements of the system, an ontology of the overall system is created. The overall ontology is complemented with domain-specific ontologies for each engineering domain. The system ontology is linked to the domain-specific ontologies by means of influence relationships enabling us to reason about relationships between system and domain-specific properties and thus also about contracts. For example, Fig. 4 shows the ontology (right side) and the different contracts (left side) of the power window system. We can clearly distinguish three areas: (a) a control area in the upper part, (b) a mapping area in the middle and (c) a hardware area in the lower part. The following subsections discuss these areas in more detail and how there are related to each other in a Contract-Based Design process consisting out of three phases: (a) negotiation, (b) deriving the domain contracts and (c) refinement of the domain contracts.

Phase 1 - Negotiation

A co-design engineering process, supported by Contract-Based Design, starts with a negotiation phase where the involved engineering domains discuss the system properties which need to hold. Therefore, each engineer represents the architecture of its domain given the system requirements. For example, the control engineer reasons about: (a) the amount of software components, (b) their in- and outputs, (c) connections between components, etc. On the other hand, the hardware engineer responsible for the hardware part of the system reasons about: (a) the number of Electronic Control Units (ECUs), (b) their processor, (c) communication between the ECUs, etc. These architectural parameters can also be ranged values. An example of such an architecture is shown in Fig. 2 which, indeed, is a refinement of the system.

Given the architecture of the involved domains and the system requirements (e.g. Table 1), the engineers decide how these architectures are related to each other. For example, when focusing on control and hardware components, they decide how the control algorithm is mapped to the hardware. In the case of the

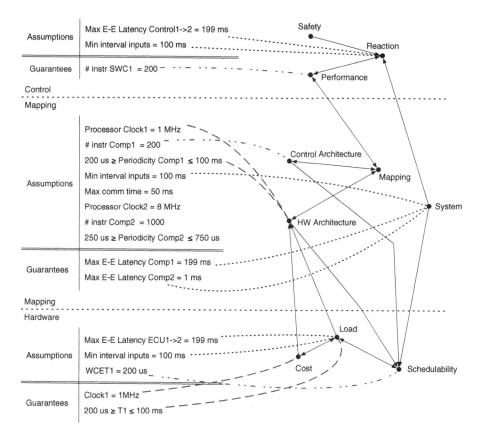

Fig. 4. Fragment of the mapping contract and the derived engineering contracts for the power window example

power window, they decide on a one-to-one mapping between a control and ECU component. Based on this mapping, a mapping contract, as shown on the left side of Fig. 4, is defined that consists out of a set of assumptions and guarantees. Properties related to the architectures are best guesses. Therefore, they are assumptions of the mapping contract. Examples of such estimated properties are: clock speed, number of instructions, periodicity, minimum interval times of the inputs, maximum communication time between ECUs, etc.

Keeping in mind the defined architectures, the given system requirements are translated to system properties as well. For example, one requirement of the power window example states that '*the power window should start moving within 200 ms after a command is issued*'. This maximum latency is refined into two guarantees of the mapping contract: (a) a maximum latency of 199 ms for mapping component 1 and (b) a maximum latency of 1 ms for mapping component 2. A mapping component refers to the one-to-one mapping of a control to an ECU component. It might be clear that the system requirements, such as these latencies, are considered as guarantees of the mapping contract. As we notice, the mapping contract as shown in Fig. 4 is a refinement of the system contract shown in Table 1. As a result, Eqs. 1–3 are valid.

Phase 2 - Deriving the Domain Contracts

In the second phase of the process, the elements of the mapping contract are subdivided into three categories using the ontology shown on the right of Fig. 4: (a) Control architecture, (b) Hardware architecture and (c) System. Based on this categorization it is decided if a contract element should be an assumption or a guarantee of the domain contract. Moreover, due to relations there exist between the ontological properties, it is decided whether a certain element is relevant for the domain contract and how it should be translated. The decision whether a contract element is translated to the domain contract is relevant when one wants to focus on one particular (extra-)functional requirement (e.g. timing, safety, etc.).

Contract elements which are related to a certain architecture become part of the guarantees of the domain contract related to that architecture. Given the mapping contract in Fig. 4, for example, the element *Processor Clock* and *Periodicity of Component 1* are translated as guaranteed elements of the hardware contract as these are design decisions the hardware engineer should take care of. Likewise, the element *Number of instructions for Component 1* is translated as a guaranteed element of the control contract. Indeed, the control engineer is responsible for maintaining this limited amount of instructions which can be influenced by the order of the control algorithm.

Contract elements which are related to the system requirement, i.e. which are part of the system contract or which are a refinement of them, are translated as assumed elements of all the involved domain contracts. Based on these assumptions, domain engineers are able to make domain specific decisions in phase 3 of the design process. Those decisions are again the guarantees of their domain contracts.

Note that every element of the mapping contract is translated to at least one domain contract over the ontological relations such that completeness is guaranteed.

Phase 3 - Refinement of the Domain Contracts

As a final phase of the co-design engineering process, the domain engineers extend and refine their own contracts, keeping in mind Eqs. 1–3, as shown in Fig. 5. For example, the hardware engineer might decide to strengthen the periodicity of component 1, i.e. increase the periodicity from 100 ms to 50 ms. He is allowed to refine this contract element since it is a design parameter he has to guarantee. However, the refinement has to be taken under the given assumptions which might be relaxed (e.g. decreasing the *maximum end-to-end latency*).

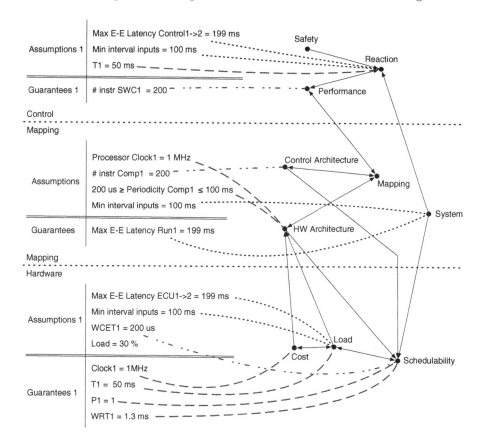

Fig. 5. Fragment of the refined engineering contracts for the power window example

Once a contract element is refined in one domain, the changes must be pushed to related contract elements which are part of the other domain contracts. This is made possible because every contract element is linked to an ontological property which in turn are related to each other by means of influence relationships. For example, the refinement of the periodicity in the hardware contract results in an update of the assumed periodicity in the control contract via the ontological properties: Load → HW Architecture → Mapping → Performance → Reaction.

7   Conclusions and Future Work

The application of contract-based design in a concurrent engineering setting with multi-disciplinary teams is not well supported. Contracts contain elements that might be irrelevant for the engineer. Furthermore, there is no clear distinction between what is assumed from other domains and what is guaranteed under these conditions.

By combining the theory of CBD with the principles of ontological reasoning, we propose a three phased process that starts with a negotiation phase. A negotiation allows engineers to discuss a common mapping contract. Using an ontology, elements of the mapping contract are translated to domain-specific contract elements and, depending on the engineering, are defined in the assumption or guarantee part of the domain contract. By definition, our methodology ensures that what is assumed in one domain will be guaranteed by another domain. Furthermore, using ontological reasoning our methodology ensures consistency between contracts and as such keeps them synchronized at all times.

It might be clear that the applicability in an industrial context is only feasible when our methodology is supported by a user-friendly tool. Given an ontology, build by a system engineer, and the negotiated mapping contract we believe the supported tool should hide phase 2 and 3 of our proposed methodology allowing engineers to focus on their core business (i.e. designing the system). Providing this tool support is considered as future work. Once available, it will allow us to increase the complexity of the use case and investigate the feasibility of our methodology on models used in industry. Besides providing tool support, we are planning to verify the compatibility of our proposed design methodology with the current state-of-the-art contract operators. We believe an extension of the current contract operators is needed to support our vision of a mapping operator which assures that all the information is put forward to the (derived) domain contracts.

Acknowledgments. This work has been carried out within the MBSE4Mechatronics project (grant nr. 130013) of the Flanders Innovation & Entrepreneurship agency (VLAIO). This research was partially supported by Flanders Make vzw.

References

1. Derler, P., Lee, E., Sangiovanni-Vincentelli, A.: Modeling cyber-physical systems. Proc. IEEE **100**(1), 13–28 (2012)
2. Lee, E.: Cyber Physical Systems: Design Challenges. In: ISORC 2008, pp. 363–369 (2008)
3. Törngren, M., Qamar, A., Biehl, M., Loiret, F., El-khoury, J.: Integrating viewpoints in the development of mechatronic products. Mechatronics **24**(7), 745–762 (2014)
4. Benveniste, A., Caillaud, B., Nickovic, D., Passerone, R., Raclet, J.-B., Reinkemeier, P., Sangiovanni-Vincentelli, A., Damm, W., Henzinger, T., Larsen, K.G.: Contracts for Systems Design, Technical report RR-8147, INRIA (2012)
5. Derler, P., Lee, E.A., Tripakis, S., Törngren, M.: Cyber-physical system design contracts. In: ICCPS 2013, pp. 109–118. ACM (2013)
6. Sangiovanni-Vincentelli, A., Damm, W., Passerone, R.: Taming Dr. Frankenstein: contract-based design for cyber-physical systems. Eur. J. Control **18**(3), 217–238 (2012)
7. Vanherpen, K., Denil, J., Dávid, I., De Meulenaere, P., Mosterman, P.J., Törngren, M., Qamar, A., Vangheluwe, H.: Ontological reasoning for consistency in the design of cyber-physical systems. In: CPPS 2016, pp. 1–8 (2016)

8. Meyer, B.: Eiffel: a language and environment for software engineering. J. Syst. Softw. **8**(3), 199–246 (1988)
9. Meyer, B.: Applying 'design by contract. Computer **25**(10), 40–51 (1992)
10. Damm, W.: Controlling speculative design processes using rich component models. In: ACSD 2005, pp. 118–119 (2005)
11. Damm, W., Votintseva, A.: Boosting re-use of embedded automotive applications through rich components. In: Proceedings of FIT, pp. 1–18 (2005)
12. Josko, B., Ma, Q., Metzner, A.: Designing embedded systems using heterogeneous rich components. INCOSE **18**(1), 558–576 (2008)
13. Benvenuti, L., Ferrari, A., Mazzi, E., Sangiovanni-Vincentelli, A.L.: Contract-based design for computation and verification of a closed-loop hybrid system. In: Egerstedt, M., Mishra, B. (eds.) HSCC 2008. LNCS, vol. 4981, pp. 58–71. Springer, Heidelberg (2008). doi:10.1007/978-3-540-78929-1_5
14. Passerone, R., Damm, W., Hafaiedh, I.B., Graf, S., Ferrari, A., Mangeruca, L., Benveniste, A., Josko, B., Peikenkamp, T., Cancila, D., Cuccuru, A., Gérard, S., Terrier, F., Sangiovanni-Vincentelli, A.: Metamodels in Europe: languages, tools, and applications. IEEE Des. Test Comput. **26**(3), 38–53 (2009)
15. OMG, A UML Profile for MARTE (version beta 1). Object Management Group, omg document number: ptc/07-08-04 ed. (2007)
16. Balarin, F., Watanabe, Y., Hsieh, H., Lavagno, L., Passerone, C., Sangiovanni-Vincentelli, A.: Metropolis: an integrated electronic system design environment. Computer **36**(4), 45–52 (2003)
17. Benveniste, A., Caillaud, B., Ferrari, A., Mangeruca, L., Passerone, R., Sofronis, C.: Multiple viewpoint contract-based specification and design. In: de Boer, F.S., Bonsangue, M.M., Graf, S., Roever, W.-P. (eds.) FMCO 2007. LNCS, vol. 5382, pp. 200–225. Springer, Heidelberg (2008). doi:10.1007/978-3-540-92188-2_9
18. Benveniste, A., Caillaud, B., Nickovic, D., Passerone, R., Raclet, J.-B., Reinkemeier, P., Sangiovanni-Vincentelli, A., Damm, W., Henzinger, T., Larsen, K.G.: Contracts for Systems Design: Methodology and Application cases. Technical report RR-8760, INRIA (2015)
19. Benveniste, A., Caillaud, B., Nickovic, D., Passerone, R., Raclet, J.-B., Reinkemeier, P., Sangiovanni-Vincentelli, A., Damm, W., Henzinger, T., Larsen, K.G.: Contracts for Systems Design: Theory. Technical report RR-8759, INRIA (2015)
20. Graf, S., Passerone, R., Quinton, S.: Contract-based reasoning for component systems with rich interactions. In: Sangiovanni-Vincentelli, A., Zeng, H., Di Natale, M., Marwedel, P. (eds.) Embedded Systems Development. Embedded Systems, vol. 20, pp. 139–154. Springer, New York (2014)
21. Nuzzo, P., Xu, H., Ozay, N., Finn, J.B., Sangiovanni-Vincentelli, A.L., Murray, R.M., Donzé, A., Seshia, S.A.: A contract-based methodology for aircraft electric power system design. IEEE Access **2**, 1–25 (2014)
22. Nuzzo, P., Sangiovanni-Vincentelli, A.L., Bresolin, D., Geretti, L., Villa, T.: A platform-based design methodology with contracts and related tools for the design of cyber-physical systems. Proc. IEEE **103**(11), 2104–2132 (2015)
23. Persson, M., Törngren, M., Qamar, A., Westman, J., Biehl, M., Tripakis, S., Vangheluwe, H., Denil, J.: A characterization of integrated multi-view modeling in the context of embedded and cyber-physical systems. In: EMSOFT 2013, pp. 1–10. IEEE Press (2013)
24. Prabhu, S.M., Mosterman, P.J.: Model-based design of a power window system: modeling, simulation, and validation. In: Society for Experimental Machines IMAC Conference (2004)

CPS Specifier – A Specification Tool for Safety-Critical Cyber-Physical Systems

Jonas Westman[1(✉)], Mattias Nyberg[1], and Oscar Thydén[2]

[1] Royal Institute of Technology (KTH), Stockholm, Sweden
jowestm@kth.se
[2] Scania, Södertälje, Sweden

Abstract. CPS Specifier is a specification tool for Cyber-Physical Systems. Founded on established theory and realized using general design and integration technologies and principles, e.g. Linked Data, CPS Specifier provides guidance- and feedback-driven support when authoring structured specifications in general, and for specifying and structuring requirements, in particular. The provided support is crucial in order to comply with functional safety standards such as IEC 61508 and ISO 26262 that require particularly stringent requirements engineering.

1 Introduction

Requirements Engineering (RE) [8] is a well-established and recommended practice within the field of systems engineering. RE is particularly emphasized in *functional safety*, where the general standard IEC 61508 [9] advocates that *safety requirements* are to form the backbone of a structured argumentation for that a system is (functionally) safe. Functional safety is a key property of *Cyber-Physical Systems* [12], e.g. a modern automotive vehicle.

In IEC 61508 and its derivative standards such as ISO 26262 [10] for the automotive domain, the argumentation over safety requirements is to be structured in an hierarchical manner in accordance with the *system architecture* [11]; at each level, safety requirements are to be *allocated* to *architecture elements* with well-defined *interfaces*. The intended property characterized by the requirement levels is to achieve *completeness*, i.e. that *"the safety requirements at one level fully implement all safety requirements of the previous level"* [10]. This is a property that also must be verified, thus, a high degree of *stringency* is required when formulating requirements and linking them together to structure a hierarchy.

Despite the highly stringent RE advocated in functional safety standards, requirements in industry is typically of poor quality [1]. Considering a typical RE tool such as IBM Rational DOORS, other than basic impact analyzes, the tool neither gives feedback nor guides a user when specifying and structuring requirements; thus, a property such as completeness must be established without any concrete support from the tool. The view in [14], which is shared in the present paper, is that RE is a complex and error-prone process that can benefit from more intelligent tool support in general. In fact, in order to comply with functional safety standards that require a particularly stringent RE,

© Springer International Publishing AG 2017
C. Berger et al. (Eds.): CyPhy 2016, LNCS 10107, pp. 116–125, 2017.
DOI: 10.1007/978-3-319-51738-4_9

tool support, which gives feedback to and guides the user when *specifying* and *structuring* requirements, is crucial.

Therefore, the present paper describes a tool called *CPS specifier*, providing such support not only when specifying and structuring requirements, but rather when *authoring* structured *specifications* for CPS in general. As the main contribution, the present paper describes how CPS Specifier provides feedback and guides the user, when:

  (i) allocating specifications and requirements to architecture elements;
 (ii) specifying interfaces of architecture elements;
(iii) specifying requirements semi-formally or formally; and
(iv) structuring requirements (specified informally, semi-formally, or formally).

This user feedback and guidance are well-founded on a general and formal requirements- and architecture-specification theory, namely established *CPS contracts theory* [2,16]; hence, the provided support is guaranteed to be sound.

The well-founded support provided by CPS Specifier for use cases (i)–(iv) is not provided by other RE tools, see e.g. [1,4,6,7] similar to CPS Specifier or [5] for a survey. For example, while CPS Specifier provides feedback and guidance for specifying requirements semi-formally and formally, tool [6] instead provides feedback on requirements specified *informally*, considering e.g. text length and consistent use of terms. Thus, CPS Specifier and [6] focus on different use cases and complement each other. This also holds true for [4] and [7] that do not focus on use cases (i)–(iv), but rather on transformation between requirements specified in different formalisms. In contrast to formal requirements analysis tools, e.g. Rodin [1], CPS Specifier offers guidance and feedback even when requirements are not specified formally, which is required in such tools. CPS Specifier does not provide full analysis support for requirements specified formally; for full support, CPS Specifier should be used in parallel with a tool such as Rodin [1].

2   Working Example and CPS Contracts Theory

This section describes Fuel Level Display (FLD), a safety-critical system installed on all trucks manufactured by Scania, with a functionality to provide an estimate of the fuel volume in the fuel tank to the driver. FLD will be described in terms of the concepts *architecture* and *contract structure*, which are formally defined in *CPS contracts theory* [2,16]. Formal definitions will not be given in the present paper; however, Sect. 4 will describe how CPS Specifier relies on these definitions to realize some of its novel features.

Architecture. This section presents an *architecture* of the FLD system as shown in Fig. 1a, i.e. in accordance with [16], a decomposition of FLD into parts, each represented as an *element* $\mathbb{E} = (X, \mathsf{B})$ with an *interface* X consisting of *port variables* and a *behavior* B, i.e. a set of *traces* [3] over the port variables in X.

In Fig. 1a, the rectangles filled with gray and the boxes on their edges represent the elements in the architecture and their port variables, respectively, and

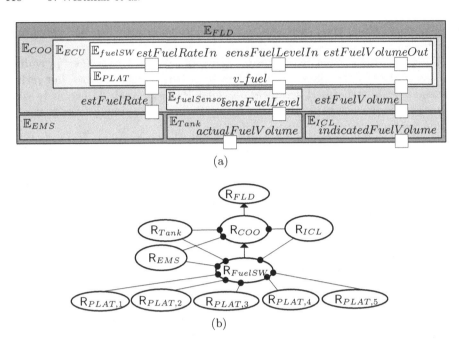

Fig. 1. (a) and (b) shows an architecture of FLD and its safety requirements organized as contract structure, respectively.

where *a shared port variable* is represented either by connecting boxes with a line or by the same box being present on several edges of rectangles. The fact that a rectangle representing an element $\mathbb{E}'$ is within another rectangle representing an element $\mathbb{E}$, represents that $\mathbb{E}'$ is a sub-element of $\mathbb{E}$.

As shown in Fig. 1a, FLD $\mathbb{E}_{FLD}$ consists of a fuel tank $\mathbb{E}_{Tank}$ and three ECU (Electric Control Unit)-systems, i.e. an ECU with sensors and actuators: Engine Management System (EMS) $\mathbb{E}_{EMS}$; Instrument CLuster (ICL) $\mathbb{E}_{ICL}$; and COOrdinator (COO) $\mathbb{E}_{COO}$. In turn, $\mathbb{E}_{COO}$ is composed of a fuel sensor $\mathbb{E}_{fuelSensor}$ and an ECU $\mathbb{E}_{ECU}$, which consists of an application software (SW) component $\mathbb{E}_{FuelSW}$ and a platform $\mathbb{E}_{PLAT}$, i.e. ECU hardware (HW) and infrastructure SW, which $\mathbb{E}_{FuelSW}$ executes on. Due to space restrictions, only a breakdown of one ECU-system is considered and this breakdown is also limited; see [16] for a more complete architecture.

The element $\mathbb{E}_{COO}$ estimates the fuel volume *actualFuelVolume*[%] in the tank $\mathbb{E}_{Tank}$ by a Kalman filter that is implemented by $\mathbb{E}_{fuelSW}$. The platform $\mathbb{E}_{PLAT}$ is to ensure that the inputs *estFuelRateIn[l/h]* and *sensFuelLevelIn*[%] and output *estFuelVolumeOut*[%] to $\mathbb{E}_{FuelSW}$ correspond to the inputs *estFuelRate[l/h]* and *sensFuelLevel*[%] and output *estFuelVolume*[%] of $\mathbb{E}_{COO}$, respectively. The port variable *sensFuelLevel*[%] represents the position of a floater in the fuel tank $\mathbb{E}_{FuelTank}$, as sensed by the fuel sensor $\mathbb{E}_{fuelSensor}$ and *estFuelRate[l/h]* is an estimate of the current rate of fuel injected into the engine and is a Controller Area Network (CAN) signal, transmitted in CAN message *FuelEconomy* from $\mathbb{E}_{EMS}$. The estimated fuel volume is transmitted as the CAN signal *estFuelVolume*[%] in CAN message *DashDisplay*. This CAN message is received by $\mathbb{E}_{ICL}$ where a fuel gauge *indicatedFuelVolume*[%] in the display presents the information to the driver.

Contract Structure. In CPS contracts theory [2,16], a *requirement* R is formalized in the same way as element behavior, i.e. as a set of traces over port variables; thus, a requirement can be specified *formally* as e.g. a relation on time-dependent port variables. A requirement specified *semi-formally* will in the following be considered to be free text with formal references to port variables. As an example of a requirement specified semi-formally, the overall safety requirement R_{FLD} on FLD can be specified as:

'*indicatedFuelVolume*[%], shown by the fuel gauge, is less than or equal to *actualFuelVolume*[%]'.

Figure 1b shows a graph where the nodes represent requirements structured in accordance with the architecture shown in Fig. 1a. Each requirement is a *safety requirement*, i.e. a requirement that has been assigned with a Safety Integrity Level (SIL) [9,10]. The subscript of each safety requirement denotes which element the requirement is *allocated* to, e.g. R_{FLD} is allocated to $\mathbb{E}_{FLD}$. The graph is a *contract structure*, introduced in [16] and extended with SILs in [15].

In CPS contracts theory, *an allocation of a requirement R to an element* is characterized by a *contract* $(\{R_1, \ldots, R_N\}, R)$ where R is called the *guarantee* and where each R_i is a requirement called an *assumption of* R. The contract expresses that the behavior of the element is to ensure that the requirement R is fulfilled given that each assumption R_i of R is fulfilled.

The fact that a requirement R' is an assumption of another requirement R is in Fig. 1b represented by an arc, called an *assume link*, from R' to R where the arc has a circle filled with black at the end. For example, R_{ICL} is an assumption of R_{fuelSW}. The safety requirement R_{ICL} is allocated to $\mathbb{E}_{ICL}$ and can be specified semi-formally as '*indicatedFuelVolume*[%] corresponds to *estFuelVolume*[%]'.

The arcs that are not assume links in Fig. 1b, i.e. those with an arrow at the end, are called *fulfill links* and represent the intent to establish *completeness* between requirement levels. More specifically, the intent is that each requirement R, which is allocated to a non-leaf architecture *element* $\mathbb{E}$, is *fulfilled* by the requirements that have fulfill links to R and are allocated to sub elements of $\mathbb{E}$. For example, the fulfill link from R_{fuelSW} to R_{COO} represent the intent that R_{fuelSW} fulfills R_{COO}.

3   CPS Specifier Design and Integration

This section presents the principles and technologies used in the overall design of CPS Specifier and its integration into the industrial tool chain at Scania. These principles and technologies enable the main contribution that will be presented in Sect. 4, i.e. the feedback- and guidance-driven support for use cases (i)–(iv).

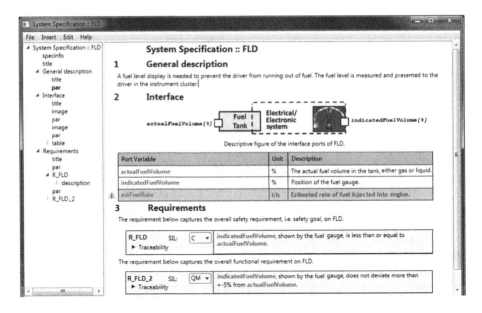

Fig. 2. Snapshot of the main window of the UI of CPS Specifier.

Design. The main window of the User Interface (UI) of CPS Specifier is shown in Fig. 2 and appears as a specification authored in a typical text editor, e.g. MS Word, with sections, free text, images, and tables; only the requirements, enclosed in rectangles filled with gray, appear differently. However, in contrast to a typical text editor, the specification content that is shown to the user is structured as machine-readable data. This machine-readable data takes the form of two different kinds, namely *implementation* and *specification data*.

Implementation data *describes* a CPS in terms of its constituent elements and interface port variables in accordance with the concept of *architecture* as presented in Sect. 2. Specification data *specifies* the CPS in terms of its intended architecture, free text descriptions, and the requirements on the CPS and their organization as a *contract structure* as also described in Sect. 2.

While the user can input specification data directly, implementation data cannot be entered directly. Instead, the user is to input a *reference* to the implementation data, whereas CPS Specifier then automatically consumes this data and presents it in the specification; input of specification data references is done in the same manner. Implementation data references are in CPS Specifier highlighted in green, e.g. in the table shown in Fig. 2, *actualFuelVolume* is an implementation reference.

Integration. The integration of CPS Specifier into the tool chain at Scania is shown in Fig. 3 where arrows represent flow of data and where tools/aspects preexisting the integration and new tools/aspects of the tool chain are color-coded with gray and white, respectively. Despite being presented in a specific context, the considered principles and technologies are applicable in a general

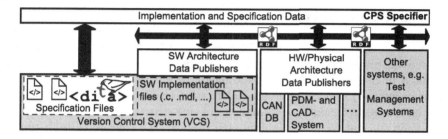

Fig. 3. Integration of CPS Specifier into the industrial tool chain at Scania.

CPS development setting, thus, allowing an arbitrary CPS developer to design and integrate a tool like CPS Specifier into its own tool chain.

CPS Specifier saves and loads specifications as XML-files in accordance with Darwin Information Typing Architecture (DITA) – an open standard for authoring specifications and publishing them as e.g. PDF-documents. Specification files are stored in the preexisting version control system (VCS) along with *SW implementation files*, i.e. source code files (e.g. .c-files) and files (e.g. Simulink .mdl files) that generate source code. Relying on preexisting VCS allows versions of specifications and SW to automatically coevolve since new versions of specifications are automatically created whenever SW development is branched/merged.

The specification files only stores data that is entered directly into a specification, referenced specification and implementation data is instead stored as references. Referenced data is consumed by CPS Specifier whenever a specification file, containing data references, is loaded; this ensures that the referenced data, presented in CPS Specifier, is *updated* and *consistent*.

A key concept for enabling this type of referencing and data interchange is Linked Data [13], which requires a standardized model for data interchange. As shown in Fig. 3, CPS Specifier uses Resource Description Framework (RDF) [13] as a standardized model for publishing and consuming data according to Linked Data. While tools such as test management systems consume data published by CPS Specifier, the tool itself consumes implementation data from *architecture data publishers*, i.e. tools that publish SW/HW/physical architecture data.

Regarding publishers of SW architecture data, the publishers automatically analyze and extract data directly from SW implementation files in the version control system using *architecture recovery* [17]. For example, SW variables and the functions that read and write to them are extracted from parsing .c-code files. Relying on architecture recovery ensures that the published data is *consistent* with the implementation.

In a similar manner, HW/physical architecture publishers automatically analyze and extract data from: the Product Data Management (PDM) system, which lists the components present in a particular vehicle; databases, e.g. CAN-DB, which lists CAN messages and signals; and other sources, e.g. Simulink models, Excel-files that describes properties of sensors and actuators, and CAD (Computer Aided Design)-systems.

4   Using CPS Specifier

This section describes how to use CPS Specifier with a focus on the main contribution of the present paper, i.e., the feedback and guidance given for the use cases presented in Sect. 1: (i) allocating specifications and requirements to architecture elements; (ii) specifying interfaces of architecture elements; (iii) specifying requirements semi-formally or formally; and (iv) structuring requirements.

A main concept used for enabling such support, is a concept called a *context of a specification*, which defines the architecture and specification data that can be referenced from different parts of the specification. In accordance with the restrictions imposed by the specification context, CPS Specifier supports input of data references using *auto-complete functionality*. Figure 4 shows an example where a list of port variables appear as possible references when specifying the safety requirement R_{fuelSW}.

(i) Allocating Specifications and Requirements to Architecture Elements. Creating a specification in CPS Specifier is created from a template with predefined sections and/or tables. Similar to a typical text editor, sections and tables, and also images and equations (in the input form of latex) can be removed or embedded in free text simply by inserting them from the menu.

Before doing any authoring, the user is first prompted with the option to select, from a list of architecture elements found in the architecture data, the architecture element that the specification is allocated to, which also determines where *the requirements* in the specification are to be allocated. For example, the specification in Fig. 2 is allocated to $\mathbb{E}_{FLD}$, which means that the two requirements R_{FLD} and $R_{FLD,2}$ in Fig. 2 are both allocated to $\mathbb{E}_{FLD}$. Notably, the user is free to not initially selecting an element for allocation; this can be done at any other time by selecting this option in the menu.

Creating a specification from a template enables CPS Specifier to *guide* the user when allocating a specification by restricting the list of architecture elements that the specification can be allocated to. For example, in the FLD case, after selecting a template for Application SW components, the list would

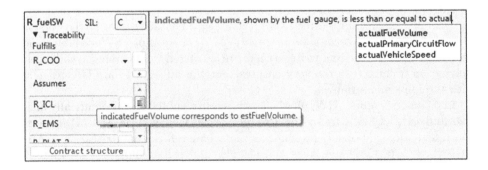

Fig. 4. Snapshot of requirement in CPS Specifier.

include $\mathbb{E}_{FuelSW}$, but exclude elements such as $\mathbb{E}_{COO}$ and $\mathbb{E}_{FuelTank}$. As will be explained further in this section, CPS Specifier will also give *feedback* on specified interfaces and requirements, and also established requirement links, immediately after allocating a specification.

(ii) Specifying Interfaces of Architecture Elements. In the specification shown in Fig. 2, there is a table listing interface port variables and their properties; this is a special table, called an *interface table*, which can be inserted from the menu.

In general, a specification can have several interface tables, typically one for each port variable type, e.g. CAN-signals, sensor inputs, etc. Content can be manually entered into these tables; however, given that the specification is allocated to an element $\mathbb{E}$, CPS Specifier will give *feedback* to the user if the listed port variables and their properties are not consistent with the architecture data consumed by CPS Specifier. An example is shown in Fig. 2 where the user is warned that the port variable *estFuelRate* is not a port variable of $\mathbb{E}_{FLD}$ according to the architecture data.

To support the user in achieving consistency, instead of entering content in an interface table manually, the user can input references to port variables in the architecture data using the auto-complete functionality; CPS Specifier will then automatically also consume and present properties of the referenced port variables. To also *guide* the user in doing this, the context of the specification will restrict the auto-complete functionality to the port variables listed as interface port variables of $\mathbb{E}$ in the architecture data. Additionally, there is an option to automatically populate interface tables with references to the interface port variables in the architecture data, thus ensuring consistency and saving much manual and error-prone work.

(iii) Specifying Requirements Semi-Formally or Formally. Requirements can be specified by inserting them from the menu; upon insertion, a unique ID is generated. Other than the ID, a SIL can be optionally entered. The user is free to specify a requirement as seen fit, even images and equations can be embedded, however, as previously mentioned and as shown in Fig. 4, explicit support is given for specifying requirements *semi-formally*, i.e. as free text with references to interface port variables, using the auto-complete functionality restricted by the specification context.

Considering such restrictions on specifying a requirement, the port variables that can be referenced in the requirement are in accordance with conditions, called *scoping* conditions, in CPS contract theory [2, 16]. Specifically, given that the requirement is allocated to an element $\mathbb{E}$ in an architecture, these conditions express that the referenced port variables must be in the union of the interfaces of the sub-elements of each proper ancestor of $\mathbb{E}$. For example, these conditions are violated if e.g. the SW variable *estFuelVolumeOut* is referenced in the safety requirement R_{FLD}, allocated to $\mathbb{E}_{FLD}$. Notably, these scoping restrictions do not only apply to requirements specified semi-formally, but also when requirements are specified *formally* as e.g. mathematical relations on port variables.

The scoping restrictions imposed by the specification context can both *guide* and *give feedback* to the user. The former since the auto-complete functionality considers the restrictions imposed the context. The latter since the user will, directly after a specification is allocated, get notified if requirements, specified prior to the allocation, now violates the scoping restrictions.

(iv) Structuring Requirements. As exemplified in Fig. 4, for a requirement R in a specification, there is a fold-down menu for creating assume and fulfill links between R and other requirements in accordance with a contract structure, as described in Sect. 2. Specifically, sources for assume links and targets for fulfill link of R can be selected from a list; hovering over a requirement in this list and the requirement is displayed, as exemplified in Fig. 4 for the requirement R_{ICL}. As shown in Fig. 4, there is also a button "contract structure" that opens up a window where R is shown in the context of a graph such as the one in Fig. 1b.

Given that the specification has been allocated to an architecture element $\mathbb{E}$, CPS Specifier will *guide* the user in establishing links between R and other requirements by restricting the set of requirements, shown as possible assume link sources and fulfill link targets, in these lists. This restriction is imposed by the specification context that enforces the definition of a contract structure. For example, none of the requirements $R_{PLAT,1}, \ldots, R_{PLAT,5}$ will appear as possible fulfill link targets of R_{fuelSW} since each $R_{PLAT,i}$ is allocated to $\mathbb{E}_{PLAT}$, to which $\mathbb{E}_{fuelSW}$ is not a sub element of.

Furthermore, similar to when specifying requirements, directly after a specification is allocated, the user will get immediate *feedback* on whether or not requirements links, established prior to allocating the specification, are in accordance with the restrictions of the specification context after the allocation.

5   Conclusion

This paper has presented CPS Specifier – a tool for authoring structured specifications for CPS. By relying on established CPS contracts theory and general design and integration technologies and principles, e.g. Linked Data, this paper has shown that CPS Specifier provides guidance and feedback for use cases (i)–(iv), which are relevant for industry in general, and for complying with functional safety standards, in particular.

In contrast to the provided support for structuring requirements, it is required that requirements are specified semi-formally or formally in order to get support when specifying requirements. However, with the use of the guided auto-complete functionality for input of implementation references, moving from specifying requirements informally to semi-formally is straightforward. Notably, moving to specifying requirements semi-formally from informally also allows powerful analyzes over specification and implementation data to answer queries such as 'what requirements are enforced on my CAN-signal or SW-variable?'.

Furthermore, it has been shown that input of implementation data references, not just in requirements, but also in e.g. interface tables, allows CPS Specifier to enforce specifications to be updated and consistent with implementation data. Thus, not only does CPS Specifier provide crucial support for specifying and structuring requirements in order to comply with functional safety standards, but it also provides support for increasing the quality of specifications in general.

References

1. Abrial, J.R., et al.: Rodin: an open toolset for modelling and reasoning in Event-B. Int. J. Softw. Tools Technol. Transf. **12**(6), 447–466 (2010)
2. Benveniste, A., Caillaud, B., Ferrari, A., Mangeruca, L., Passerone, R., Sofronis, C.: Multiple viewpoint contract-based specification and design. In: Boer, F.S., Bonsangue, M.M., Graf, S., Roever, W.-P. (eds.) FMCO 2007. LNCS, vol. 5382, pp. 200–225. Springer, Heidelberg (2008). doi:10.1007/978-3-540-92188-2_9
3. Dill, D.L.: Trace theory for automatic hierarchical verification of speed-independent circuits. In: Proceedings of the Fifth MIT Conference on Advanced Research in VLSI, pp. 51–65. MIT Press, Cambridge (1988)
4. Farfeleder, S., et al.: DODT: increasing requirements formalism using domain ontologies for improved embedded systems development. In: IEEE International Symposium on Design and Diagnostics of Electronic Circuits and Systems, pp. 271–274 (2011)
5. de Gea, J.M.C., Nicolás, J., Alemán, J.L.F., Toval, A., Ebert, C., Vizcaíno, A.: Requirements engineering tools. IEEE Softw. **28**(4), 86–91 (2011)
6. Génova, G., et al.: A framework to measure and improve the quality of textual requirements. Requir. Eng. **18**(1), 25–41 (2013)
7. Hähnle, R., Johannisson, K., Ranta, A.: An authoring tool for informal and formal requirements specifications. In: Kutsche, R.-D., Weber, H. (eds.) FASE 2002. LNCS, vol. 2306, pp. 233–248. Springer, Heidelberg (2002). doi:10.1007/3-540-45923-5_16
8. Hull, M.E.C., et al. (eds.): Requirements Engineering, 3rd edn. Springer, London (2011)
9. IEC 61508: Functional safety of E/E/PE safety-related systems (2010)
10. ISO 26262: Road vehicles - functional safety (2011)
11. ISO/IEC/IEEE 42010: System and software engineering - architecture description (2011)
12. Rawat, D.B., Rodrigues, J.J., Stojmenovic, I.: Cyber-Physical Systems: From Theory to Practice. CRC Press, Boca Raton (2015)
13. Speicher, S., Arwe, J., Malhotra, A.: Linked data platform 1.0 (2015)
14. Sutcliffe, A., Maiden, N.: The domain theory for requirements engineering. IEEE Trans. Softw. Eng. **24**(3), 174–196 (1998)
15. Westman, J., Nyberg, M.: Extending contract theory with safety integrity levels. In: 2015 IEEE 16th International Symposium on HASE, pp. 85–92, January 2015
16. Westman, J., Nyberg, M.: Contracts for specifying and structuring requirements on cyber-physical systems. In: Rawat, D.B., Rodriques, J., Stojmenovic, I. (eds.) Cyber Physical Systems: From Theory to Practice. Taylor & Francis, Boca Raton (2015)
17. Zhang, X., et al.: Experience on applying software architecture recovery to automotive embedded systems. In: Software Maintenance, Reengineering and Reverse Engineering (CSMR-WCRE), pp. 379–382, February 2014

Author Index

Ahmad, Waheed   1

Betsuno, Kenichi   17

Caltais, Georgiana   31
Chowdhury, Shafiul Azam   46
Csallner, Christoph   46

De Meulenaere, Paul   101
Denil, Joachim   101
Dulay, Naranker   61

Glesner, Sabine   71
Göthel, Thomas   71

Herber, Paula   71
Hohmann, Sören   87
Holzmüller, Bernd   87

Johnson, Taylor T.   46

Leahy, Fergus   61
Leitner-Fischer, Florian   31
Leue, Stefan   31

Matsumoto, Shota   17

Nyberg, Mattias   116

Rensink, Arend   1

Schlesinger, Sebastian   71
Schwab, Stefan   87
Stoelinga, Mariëlle   1

Thydén, Oscar   116

Ueda, Kazunori   17

Vangheluwe, Hans   101
Vanherpen, Ken   101

Weiser, Jannis   31
Westman, Jonas   116

Yildiz, Bugra M.   1

Printed in the United States
By Bookmasters